UNIQUE EATS AND EATERIES

OF

THE PEOPLE AND STORIES BEHIND THE FOOD

Copyright © 2024 by Reedy Press, LLC
Reedy Press
PO Box 5131
St. Louis, MO 63139, USA
reedypress.com

Library of Congress Control Number: 2024939293

ISBN: 9781681065663

Design by Jill Halpin

Cover photo credits, clockwise from top: Fort Wayne's Famous Coney Island, Carrie Steinweg, Bao's Pastry, Carrie Steinweg, Little Italy.

Back cover headshot courtesy of Paul Steinweg. For back cover photo credits, see credits for these photos on their interior pages.

All title page photos are courtesy of the author except top left photo: courtesy of Bao's Pastry and top right photo: courtesy of Fort Wayne's Famous Coney Island.

All other photos are courtesy of the author unless otherwise noted.

Printed in the United States of America
24 25 26 27 28   5 4 3 2 1

UNIQUE EATS AND EATERIES

OF

THE PEOPLE AND STORIES BEHIND THE FOOD

CARRIE STEINWEG

Junk Ditch Brewing Company

DEDICATION

To Paul, my very favorite dining companion, and to my foodie sisters with whom I have shared many culinary adventures.

Also, to all of the restaurant owners, chefs, cooks, servers, sommeliers, dishwashers, busboys, hostesses, candymakers, ice cream scoopers, and other hospitality employees who pour their hearts into their work every day to bring us delicious food and cherished memories.

St. James Restaurant

CONTENTS

ACKNOWLEDGMENTS

This book couldn't have been possible without the help of several special people in my life; colleagues in the writing, tourism, and PR world; and those who keep these unique slices of culinary life running smoothly.

Thanks first of all to my hubby, Paul, for being my partner in life and in all my travel and food adventures. Dedicating time not just to write a full manuscript, but also to do countless hours of research, make many phone calls, take oodles of notes, and drive all over the state can really hijack your life for a while, and I thank him for picking up the slack and being patient as I made this book happen. My sincere gratitude to him for being my dining companion, photographer, videographer, proofreader, chauffeur, sounding board, bag carrier, plate sharer, and more—and for all the cold meals he's been subjected to while I got just the right shot. His support and love mean everything.

My favorite ginger—my son Carter—deserves a bit of gratitude for assisting in editing. Gracias, also, to my BFF, Michelle Brown, for always being an enthusiastic cheerleader in all my endeavors. Thanks also to my friend, Jeannie McCall, for lending her proofreading assistance.

To all of the CVBs and their partners who hosted me, dined with me, or put me in touch with restaurant owners and representatives: you helped immensely in making this book a reality.

And thanks to all the friends and tourism professionals who suggested eateries that I needed to visit, including Lindsey Skeen, Clare Clark, Jessa Campbell, Terry Mark, Mo Lambert, Josh Duke, Jennifer Long Dillon, Trenton Bush, Nancy Sartain, Erin White, Grace Caswell, Kristal Painter, Sonya Nash, Sara Erickson, Jordan

Smith, Amy Collier, Karen Kijewski, and especially Amy Howell with Visit Indiana, a kindred foodie spirit who loves highlighting Hoosier grub as much as I do.

And can we please insert a moment of silence here for my willpower in acknowledgement of the 10 pounds that crept on in the writing of this book—a result of tasting way too many breaded pork tenderloins, creamy soups, french fries, and sliccs of pie.

In this book, I focused mostly on small, independently owned places and sought out some of those gems that are often overlooked. Some are little mom-and-pop places that do not even have websites, so I hope that their mention in this publication will lead new guests to find their way there. I do, however, want to give a shout-out to some favorite local and regional chains that exist in or started in Indiana that have been feeding patrons for decades, among them Pizza King, Schoop's, Boz Hot Dogs, South Bend Chocolate Company, and Jack's Donuts. They're some of the spots that also contribute greatly to the Hoosier food scene and where so many memories are made.

It was a hard task narrowing down the list to a manageable number to fit on the pages of this book. There are so many more special places that are worth visiting that just couldn't fit within these pages, and I hope that this book inspires further exploration of eateries throughout the Hoosier State.

INTRODUCTION

There's no reason to ever go hungry or have a craving go unfulfilled in the Hoosier State. From the food mecca of Indianapolis to tiny eateries in small rural towns, from spots dotted along one of the Great Lakes to high-end steak houses and everything in between, there's something for everybody.

What may be regarded as simply a flyover state by those who haven't spent time in Indiana is really a beautiful tapestry of Midwestern hospitality filled with historians, sports enthusiasts, outdoor recreationists, hard workers, artisans, farmers, and more. And it's a state that doesn't quite get its earned due when it comes to the culinary landscape.

I lived much of my life so far in the Chicago suburbs, but just a stone's throw from the Indiana border where some days I spent the majority of my time across the state line, dropping my kids off to school, going to doctor or dentist appointments, shopping for groceries, filling my gas tank, attending shows and festivals—and doing lots of eating. And since becoming a full-fledged Hoosier in recent years after a move to Northwest Indiana, I'm enjoying learning more and more about my new home state—and trying more and more new restaurants.

While food in Indiana is often likened to heavy comfort food, that's just part of the story. They do heavy and hearty so well, but you'll also find a variety of amazing ethnic restaurants, some going back to early immigrant roots and some newer spots catering to growing ethnic populations in and around some of Indiana's larger cities. Farm to fork is alive and well in Indiana, where rural residents account for about 20 percent of the state's population and farmland accounts for over 60 percent of the total land.

Indiana is where products like Red Gold ketchup, Wonder Bread, Jet-Puffed marshmallows, Orville Redenbacher's popcorn, and Van Camp's pork and beans either originated or have been produced. It's also where pork tenderloin is the sandwich of the land, sugar cream is the official state pie, and an Amish-style buffet is something you have to experience.

From nostalgic diners where the waitresses know regulars by name to James Beard–nominated, elevated gastronomic experiences, you'll find it all in Indiana. And I have loved getting to know the food scene bite by bite in small towns and big cities. By the way, this book is not even close to a full list of unique eateries in the state. There's so much more, but only so many pages in a book. I hope this will inspire you to broaden your foodie horizons, take a road trip and explore, and get a taste of what Indiana has to offer.

Food brings people together. It creates cherished memories. A celebration after a high school sports win for burgers and milkshakes with jukebox music. A toast at a lively pub with good grub after your friend gets engaged. A trip with the grandkids to Amish country for fried chicken and pie and a look at life in the slow lane. Digging into a big ice cream treat on a sunny summer day at a nostalgic creamery. There are so many foodie memories to be made in Indiana. Dive in and take a bite!

UNIQUE EATS AND EATERIES

OF

INDIANA

ST. ELMO STEAK HOUSE

Home of the world-famous shrimp cocktail

If there's one place in Indiana that checks all the boxes when it comes to an ideal place to enjoy a meal on a special occasion, to sit back and chat with locals at the bar, or to just sit down to an upscale, scrumptious meat-and-potatoes meal, it's St. Elmo Steak House in Indianapolis. It's got ambiance, a romantic and fascinating history, a great downtown location, abundantly friendly staff, celebrity regulars, fabulous food, and a specialty on their appetizer menu that will bring tears to your eyes—literally.

Founded in 1902, it's the oldest steak house in Indianapolis, and the founder, Joe Stahr, named it after the patron saint of sailors, St. Elmo. It started in one corner building, the Braden's Block building, which was completed in 1875. It later expanded to two additional buildings, including the Italian-style Reinhardt Building that is the oldest surviving building in the area, dating back to 1864.

St. Elmo has been called an "institution" and has received immense praise and numerous accolades for the food, wine, service, and charm over the years from prestigious publications and organizations. In 2012 it was recognized with the America's Classics Award by the James Beard Foundation.

You'll find only one appetizer on the menu, and it's the same one that has satisfied customers since the beginning. The shrimp cocktail is legendary—a serving of four jumbo shrimp served

---

St. Elmo Steak House was named for the patron saint of sailors, St. Elmo.

Left: A neon sign lures in diners to the iconic St. Elmo Steak House, which dates back to 1902. *Right:* Longtime server Phil Starks creates a memorable dining experience, interacting with customers with humor and kindness.

with their signature spicy cocktail sauce. That unmistakable bite comes from four tons of horseradish that the restaurant goes through each year, shaving it in-house for an überhot surprise that will clear your sinuses.

You'll also want to try the navy bean soup, another original menu item still served today that went along with the sailor theme. Be sure to try their signature cocktail to accompany it: the Elmo Cola.

Situated just blocks away from Lucas Oil Stadium, the home of the Indianapolis Colts, St. Elmo is a popular spot for a postgame celebration where athletes gather. Peyton Manning was a frequent visitor during his time with the team. Private rooms in the lower level have hosted all kinds of famous names. As one server said, "One day you might walk into the dining room to see Hall and Oates looking up at the wall to find their picture, and the next day Lady Gaga is dining downstairs with the Dalai Lama."

127 S Illinois St., Indianapolis, 317-635-0636
stelmos.com

FARINA'S SUPPER CLUB

An old-school experience just off Lake Michigan

Nestled in a neighborhood that sits along the shore of Lake Michigan, Farina's Supper Club is a taste of old-school elegance and history with a kitchen brimming with phenomenal aromas of homemade pastas and sauces and a friendly atmosphere that only a classic supper club can provide.

Formerly the Duneland Beach Inn, the historic building once housed beachgoers and vacationers who came to the Duneland Beach area for its quiet, calm atmosphere and pristine natural surroundings. It was recently renovated to provide the throwback experience of luxury paired with high-quality Italian cuisine. You'll find it at Stop 33 along the Dunes, just a short walk from Lake Michigan in a tree-lined residential neighborhood.

The sophisticated restaurant has a charming patio for outdoor dining, an intimate bar area, and a cigar patio where you can lounge with a cocktail and cigar after a fine meal.

The owners, founder Yvonne Farina and cofounder and culinary director Chef Joe Farina, have a wealth of experience in the restaurant industry in the Chicago area. Joe's career began at Hotel Nikko and the Chicago Yacht Club before he became head chef at Carmine's, part of Chicago's iconic Rosebud Restaurant Group. Later, as cofounder of Victory Restaurant Group, he brought his flair for fine cuisine to Victory Tap in the South Loop, Victory Italian in River North and Oak Park, and Victory Meat & Seafood in Elmhurst.

Yvonne's passion for food, wine, and entertaining led her to a career in hospitality where she worked with some of the most legendary names in the industry in Chicago. When the two made Michigan City their new hometown, they joined to bring a new concept to this little corner of their new community.

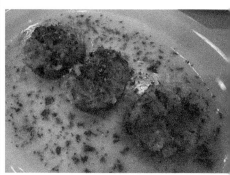

Left: Situated in a wooded neighborhood just off of the Lake Michigan lakefront, Farina's Supper Club is in a historic building that was once the Duneland Beach Inn. *Right:* The stuffed mushrooms are an irresistible appetizer of mushroom caps stuffed with parmesan herb breadcrumbs with a lemon sauce.

The decor harkens back to a century ago with flora-filled wallpaper atop white wainscoting with cozy fireplaces and candlelight. You'll find all the classics here—some with a twist, starting with the appetizers. They've got the most extraordinary take on a caprese salad—a stack of fresh mozzarella and plum tomatoes drizzled with balsamic, but with the addition of an herb-breaded eggplant. Get a nice sampling of Chef Joe's specialties with the Old Neighborhood Platter, which comes with braciola, Chef Joe's famous homemade meatballs, and Italian sausage over house-made cavatelli with tomato wine sauce.

Save room for dessert—you'll find tiramisu and cannoli that would make any nona very proud.

An impressive international wine list includes bottles from Washington and California to New Zealand, France, and Italy. You'll also have some indulgent after-dinner drinks to choose from.

3311 Pottawattomie Trl., Michigan City, 219-874-7729
farinasupperclub.com

> Meals start with house-made parmesan garlic bread served with a slow-simmered marinara sauce for dipping. The double-baked bread is made daily, buttered and topped with cheese, and baked again.

DESTINATION 814

A place of approachable sophistication

If you like to pair spirits with your meal, you might consider a visit to Destination 814 Bourbon Bar & Scratch Kitchen in LaGrange. The fairly new spot was opened in 2020 by a couple of locals, Anthony and Cheri Riegling, who had years of experience in the restaurant industry and previously owned two other restaurant-bars. It is situated in a former car dealership building that was renovated with an industrial look to accommodate crowds looking for something a notch up from a standard eatery and bar. It has a modern and upscale yet friendly vibe where you can get some down-home favorites, but with an elevated touch. Whether you want a burger, a slab of ribs, a light salad, or a high-quality steak, you can get it here. There's something for every palate. Their goal was to bring a big-city vibe to this small community.

The menu includes some booze-infused dishes—garlic butter chicken with whiskey butter mushrooms; the whiskey apple and PB burger with cheddar, bacon, whiskey apples, jalapeños and house peanut butter; the Hoosier tenderloin sandwich topped with cheddar and bourbon ham; and bourbon chicken with provolone, bourbon mushrooms, bacon, shaved onions, and bourbon sauce.

The menu has all the casual-fare faves, like burgers and sandwiches, but some with a twist. The open-faced Philly steak on Texas toast with pico de gallo is one example. There's also a large selection of elevated salads, bowls, and out-of-the-box flatbreads, like crab rangoon as one of the more interesting options.

They also offer a number of upscale seafood and steak entrées on the specials menu, some being a filet mignon over creamed spinach with fried lyonnaise potatoes or a seared cod fillet with coconut

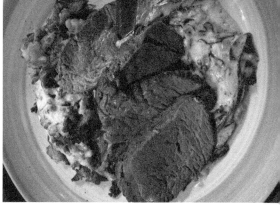

Clockwise from top left: The walls behind and shelves above the bar contain a huge variety of bourbons and other spirits that make this place stand out from other local bars. You'll find a diverse selection of seafood and steak specials on the menu, like this filet mignon served over creamed spinach with fried lyonnaise potatoes. The Hoosier Tenderloin Sandwich is topped with cheddar and bourbon ham. Be sure to try out one of their 16 whiskey flights.

Malibu rice, mango puree, and fresh mango cucumber relish. And if you are someone who is all about the sauce, you'll have your pick of some good ones when you're here. Horsey sauce goes great with some of the beef sandwiches and entrées. The beer cheese is a nice addition to sandwiches and a nice flavor to add to fries.

Aside from food, there's a wide selection of spirits, beers, and cocktails that you might not expect. You'll find bourbon options here that you probably won't find anywhere else in the county.

814 Detroit St., LaGrange, 260-214-5612
destination814bar.com

LONG'S BAKERY

You'll fall in love with their hot yeast at first bite

Bakeries often have a sweet spot in people's hearts, harkening back to memories of childhood weekends with parents or grandparents treating them to an assorted box of a dozen pieces of round sugary paradise to choose from. Long's Bakery defines childhood indulgence for so many and evokes decades of sweet reminiscences.

The business was opened on January 29, 1955, by Carl Long, and it continues nearly seven decades later by a fourth generation: Long's great granddaughter, Crystal, and her husband, Robby Smith.

The original sign still stands on the corner of 16th and Tremont in front of the bakery, luring hungry costumers in for hot "do-nuts." Little has changed at this spot in the best possible way. Everything is still made fresh daily from scratch at the same counter where generations have come for their sweet fix. New items, such as an oatmeal cream pie and a new strawberry-dipped yeast doughnut, have popped up in recent years in addition to longtime favorites.

Long's is best known for their hot yeast doughnuts. It's a simple, fried, glazed yeast doughnut that is best enjoyed when it's hot. They're made fresh throughout the day, so if you arrive at just the right time as they're being lifted from the fryer, you may be lucky enough to snag one at its absolute peak. Even cooled down, it's a treat that melts in your mouth.

> Long's is located less than two miles from the Indianapolis Motor Speedway and they made Thrillist's list of 32 Best Donut Shops in America in 2022.

Left: A vintage sign outside greets visitors to this Indianapolis baked goods staple. *Center:* Robby Smith, who currently co-owns Long's Bakery with his wife, Crystal, the great granddaughter of the founder, Carol Long, holds a box of freshly-made treats. *Top right:* The hot yeast donut is a best seller at Long's Bakery in Indianapolis. *Bottom right:* If you're looking for a unique item you can't find at any other bakery, try the Mary Ann, a cream-filled chocolate cake covered with a dollop of marshmallow and then covered in chocolate.

Smith recommends enjoying them when they are fresh. Because they have longer hours than a typical bakery, you can stop throughout the day to grab a fresh dozen whenever you get a craving. And doughnuts aren't the only thing you'll find there. Bars and brownies. Cakes and cookies. Pies and strudels. So many things that will satisfy the sweet tooth. One unique item that you'll only find at Long's is something called a Mary Ann. Think Ding Dong with a chocolate-covered marshmallow dollop on top. It's a perfect mix of chocolaty and creamy.

The original location is still cranking out sweet treats every day of the week, and they get there in the wee hours of the morning to get started. The lobby is small with room for a line to make its way through, but no room for seating so you'll have to take your treats to go. You can also enjoy treats from the second location on Southport Road.

Be sure to bring cash because they don't take credit cards. This helps them keep the costs down, according to Smith, and at the time of printing, some of their doughnuts could still be purchased for 92 cents.

They have unusual hours for a bakery and are open into the evening, from 5:30 a.m. to 10 p.m.

1453 N Tremont St., Indianapolis, 317-632-3741

8ELEVEN MODERN BISTRO

Classy hotel restaurant is an ode to astronauts

8Eleven Modern Bistro is located inside the Union Club Hotel, which sits on the campus of Purdue University in West Lafayette. In 2020 the hotel reopened after a $35 million renovation, which included opening a new culinary anchor in a modern, upscale, full-service French/American-inspired eatery named for two of NASA's most daring aerospace programs, Gemini 8 and Apollo 11.

Purdue University has played a large role in the area of space exploration, producing a total of 27 graduates who went on to become NASA astronauts, including Neil Armstrong, Roger Chafee, Gus Grissom, Eugene Cernan and Janice Voss.

The university was founded in 1869 and established as a college of science, technology and agriculture by Lafayette businessman John Purdue, who donated the land and funding. The first classes were held in 1874.

Although the style of the hotel and restaurant is modern, it also offers nods to the past in the photography, woodwork, and logos worked into the design throughout the property. The hotel first opened in 1929 as an addition to the Purdue Memorial Union.

The dining room is oozing with opulent ambiance and provides a dining experience unlike any other in the area. Open for breakfast and lunch service, it closes for a brief break before dinner service begins. Your best bet is to get a room and have a meal from each of the three menus.

The restaurant's name, 8Eleven, comes from two NASA missions commanded by Neil Armstrong, an alumnus of Purdue University.

Left: The elegant dining room and Boiler Up Bar give a feel of prestige and tradition. *Right:* Choose from a large selection of premium cocktails and wine with your meal.

Start your day with specialties like Bistro Steak & Eggs, a Spinach & Mushroom Egg White Omelet, or Smoked Salmon Toast. It's perfect for a pregame brunch if you're there to see the Boilermakers play or a leisurely outing with friends or family.

If you love burgers, try the Brush Creek Ranch Wagyu Cheeseburger, which is a half-pound of brisket blend topped with premium toppings like onion jam and gruyère.

Start out dinner with exquisite oysters, shrimp cocktail, crab croquettes, or steak tartare.

There are some impressive seafood entrées, like Ora King Salmon and Diver Scallops, flanked with exotic vegetables and creamy sauces on the menu aside a Filet Oscar; decadent pasta dishes; and hearty chicken, beef, and pork entrées.

When you get to the end of the meal, don't pass on dessert. They make some stunning pastries and sweet bites.

Even though the atmosphere is elegant, children are welcome and there's even a kids' menu. Vegetarians, vegans, and those with gluten sensitivities will find some nice options on the menu, as well.

201 S Grant St., Ste. 100, West Lafayette, 765-496-5126
8elevenbistro.com

ASPARAGUS

Ambiance, elegance, and Asian Fusion

Spend a couple hours in the dining room of Asparagus and you'll feel like you've been transported to Thailand or Vietnam. You don't go there and have a meal. You go there and have an experience. A zen-like ambiance awaits you where you can savor Asian classics and French-inspired culinary artistry, sip on wines from an extensive collection, and just escape.

Chef Tammy Pham opened her first restaurant, Siam Marina, back in 1995 in Calumet City, Illinois, and when the building was slated to be torn down, she and her husband Sam moved the restaurant to Tinley Park, Illinois, in 2014. It's still going strong today. The couple are both natives of Vietnam. In 2007, they opened their sister restaurant, Asparagus, in Merrillville and just over a year after it opened, the South Shore Convention and Visitors Authority declared it "Restaurant of the Year." It's been praised by food critics and featured on The Steve Harvey Show.

Bamboo, white tablecloths, hues of green and rich yellows, and fresh flowers help create an oasis where every bite and sip is an adventure in this Asian fusion restaurant and lounge. Asian art that has been procured by the Phams on their travels dons the walls and dining room—a collection of paintings, sculptures, and antique artifacts.

There are cold and crispy rolls for sharing filled with lobster, crabmeat, shrimp, avocado, cabbage, and more, combining veggies and proteins perfectly in a crunchy casing with delicious dips for

> **Chef Tammy Pham has bottled her Sassy Sweet & Sour Sauce, which can be purchased at the restaurant.**

Left: Asparagus offers dishes fashioned from the cuisines of Thailand, Vietnam and the Americas with French artistry. *Center:* The bar area provides a tranquil space to sit and sip on a craft cocktail. *Top right:* Fresh seafood is enhanced with a a variety of Asian-inspired flavors and presentations. *Bottom right:* You'll find a warm and spacious interior when visiting Asparagus.

dunking. It's a great place to go with friends, order several dishes, and turn it into a family-style feast. Small plates lend themselves well for that purpose—tempura dishes, ribs, meatballs, and wings are among the options.

Entrées vary from Vietnamese stew to curries to stir fries and much more, each one sounding even more flavorful than the last: fried rice and noodle dishes are must-try items, especially drunken noodles that are flavored with a touch of exotic wine.

Don't get too full, though. You haven't lived until you've had a piece of Chef Tammy's hummingbird cake.

The cocktails are in a class of their own, and although it would be a sin to not sample the food on a stop there, it's totally worthy of making the trip just for the drinks. Sam's collection of wines will also wow you.

The eatery can accommodate over 250 guests and has a 16-person private dining room. The lounge features a baby grand piano where world-class musicians perform twice a month. Sign up to get on the VIP list for secret menus, special offers, the loyalty program, and first looks at exclusive events. The cocktail events and wine pairing dinners are quite popular and sell out quickly, so be sure to jump on them when you learn one is coming up.

7876 Broadway, Merrillville, 219-794-0000
asparagusrestaurant.com

ST. JAMES RESTAURANT

Northern Indiana's oldest restaurant

Food has been served continuously at St. James Restaurant since its opening as a hotel in 1878. Built by Jonathan James, a Pennsylvania farmer who had moved to Indiana in 1860, it was purchased and revived in 1948 by Bill and Evelyn Freeman. It's one of the Midwest's oldest continually operating restaurants.

The property has seen changes over the years, with a second dining room built on the back and an enclosed porch added on. The upstairs, where guest rooms once were, is now a banquet room, but the dining room is in its original location with a new bar that was built in 1991.

The place is clean and cozy and nostalgically classy. Stained glass accents the walls and the welcoming wood bar sits beaneath coffered ceilings. The bar features detailed carvings and has the words "St. James" etched above the tappers.

The menu is full of savory, comforting dishes, hand-cut steaks, and perfectly cooked seafood, but the one standout on the menu is their broasted chicken. It's won awards and is part of the Indiana Foodways Winner, Winner Chicken Dinner culinary trail. Chicken has been on the menu since the early days, but the Freemans elevated their birds by broasting rather than frying, allowing for meat that is juicy and a batter that is crispy.

Ribs are rubbed with their St. James spice blend and hickory-smoked in-house, then served with house-made barbecue sauces. Crab cakes are another signature item made with real crab and a homemade spicy dijon. North Atlantic cod is fried in their own St. James breading.

There's a bit of a German influence in the menu, and if you're a fan of German potato salad, be sure to select it as one of the sides with your dinner. Dinner portions are very generous. If you're eating lighter, ask for the "plate."

Clockwise, from top left: Start out your visit to St. James Restaurant with an appetizer combo. The Indiana Restaurant Association has recognized St. James Restaurant as the oldest restaurant in Northern Indiana. Grab a pint at the bar of St. James, which served as a hotel, restaurant and watering hole when the businesses began in 1878. Seafood lovers will enjoy dining at St. James where Faroe Island salmon, broiled sea scallops, North Atlantic cod, cold water lobster tail and jumbo shrimp are on the menu.

A popular longtime recipe is the sauerkraut, which is now a special served each Thursday. Ham and bean and chicken noodle soups are on the menu daily. Much of the menu is scratch made, and the coleslaw is a unique version that is very finely chopped.

St. James is also a nice place to stop if you're just looking to get a drink and dessert. There are a number of craft beers on tap, with typically a couple from nearby microbreweries in their eight rotating taps. Among the signature cocktails is a Blackberry Long Island, Carribean Colada, St. James Old-Fashioned, and Famous Homemade Manhattan.

Finish off your meal with one of 15 dessert cocktails, including a Grasshopper, Brandy Alexander, or Pink Squirrel, or opt for one of the indulgent multilayer desserts or cheesecake slices.

Take time to walk around and admire the stained glass and view the historic photographs and many newspaper clippings about this famous stop.

204 E Albion St., Avilla, 260-897-2114
stjamesavilla.com

FORT WAYNE'S FAMOUS CONEY ISLAND WIENER STAND

Welcome to the country's oldest coney stand

When you've got a good thing going, why change? Fort Wayne's Famous Coney Island Wiener Stand began in 1914, bringing simple food to the working men of the city. Those simple beginnings and recipes brought from its Macedonian founders are what still bring in customers today.

Not much has changed at this hot dog joint. The layout is the same. The same barstools still seat hungry patrons. Even a McCray cooler installed in the 1920s is still in use. Historic photos hang on the walls confirming that the dining room today is kind of like a time capsule.

Since 1916, the business has remained in the same family. A third generation is half owner and the other half belongs to Jimmy Todoran, who started working at the eatery at just 15 and whose own father had worked there before he was born. Both have ensured that traditions have continued and that whether you are 5 or 95, you can still go in and get a coney dog that tastes just like the first bite you'd ever had there.

It's the oldest operating restaurant in Fort Wayne and claims to be the oldest hot dog stand in America. Harkened by the lighted sign outside, the neon sign facing out at the customers, and the draw of the hot dogs lined up on a flat grill in the window, steady streams of customers make their way in year-round. In fact, they get so busy that they open the doors at 9 a.m. seven days a week. During busy times,

---

Famous customers have included comedian Jay Leno, rock star Huey Lewis, actress Shelley Long, and Vice President Mike Pence.

Left: Hot dogs are lined up on a grill that can be viewed through the large front glass window. *Center:* Burgers are flipped on a grill at the front of the restaurant visible by those passing by on the street. *Right:* The interior of Fort Wayne's Famous Coney Island has not changed much since opening in 1914.

a line forms outside as customers wait their turn to get a seat along the counter or at one of the tables lining the wall.

Once you're inside, though, things move fast. Service is fast and friendly, and often your coney dog is placed in front of you before you even get your coat off and get comfortable.

The menu is so brief you could almost try one of everything in your first sitting. Aside from the hot dogs, you can also get hamburgers and cheeseburgers at surprisingly low prices (a burger under $5 in 2024 is a pretty rare occurrence!). You can also get a bowl of homemade chili that is prepared daily. It is made sans beans, but you can order a bowl of oven-baked beans to add into the chili or enjoy on the side. A bag of chips and a slice of pie round out the menu. That's it. Short, sweet, and simple.

But let's back up to the dogs. They are the absolute star of the show. The grilled Coney Island Hot Dog is served on a steamed bun with mustard, homemade coney sauce, and hand-chopped onions. They're satisfying, but it's not unusual to watch a guy sit down and consume four or five in just a few minutes.

Beverage choices are coffee, hot chocolate, water, or pop. You can get a fountain drink or a can of pop, but your experience isn't really complete unless you order a glass bottle of Coca-Cola. They've been serving it in the bottle since 1914.

131 W Main St., Fort Wayne, 260-424-2997
fortwaynesfamousconeyisland.com

DAS DUTCHMAN ESSENHAUS

A taste of Amish cuisine at Indiana's largest family restaurant

In 1970, Bob and Sue Miller bought an old 24-hour truck stop in the heart of Amish country in Middlebury. The couple decided to give it a makeover, remove the cigarette machine, close on Sundays, and provide the public with a meal like one they'd find in a nearby Amish home. The 150-seat eatery opened in 1971 and has grown by leaps and bounds to become the largest restaurant in the state.

In the early days, Bob would pick up his Amish help in his 1969 Malibu and bring them to work in the kitchen. Today they still have a number of Amish employees and a bus that picks them up and returns them after their shift. Using authentic recipes that are handmade and served by Amish hands gives an extra layer to the comfort food that makes its way onto the plates of diners.

If you're looking for a delicious, wholesome, stick-to-your-ribs meal, this is where you'll find it. You can choose to order off the menu; have family-style dishes brought to your table; or fill your plate at the sizable buffet of crisp, broasted chicken, creamy mashed potatoes with rich homemade gravy, freshly made noodles, and much more.

Over the years the restaurant grew to add more seating and a gift shop. The adjoining bakery became a big part of the business. Pies are a big deal, and you'll find about 30 different varieties to choose from, with popular favorites like red raspberry cream, old-fashioned cream, Dutch apple, and praline pecan cream; seasonal flavors like fresh peach, strawberry rhubarb crumb, and pumpkin; and less common flavors like mincemeat and shoofly.

Left: While waiting for a table or after your meal, be sure to take time do some some shopping for gift items, dishes, baked goods, jams and more. *Center: Campus Manager Joel Miller is pictured with the restaurant's longest-serving employee, Sharon Frye, who started there in 1973. Right:* Customers at Das Dutchman Essenhaus will enjoy a hearty plate of Amish-style cooking.

In the bakery, you can get many of their other homemade items, like apple butter, cookies, cinnamon rolls, peanut butter, salad dressing, and their noodles. The noodles became so popular that they are now distributed in grocery stores across the country and there was a need to add a facility across the street that produces nothing but noodles. It has since expanded, enabling Essenhaus to produce double the amount of noodles in the same amount of time.

The holidays are an ideal time to visit when the restaurant is all decked out for the season.

The restaurant is part of a 130-acre campus with a hotel and conference center, quaint shops, mini golf, gardens, and more. Car cruise-ins are also held there in the warmer months, drawing up to 1,800 cars in a night. An annual train show draws in train collectors and enthusiasts from all over.

There are also five Das Dutchman Essenhaus restaurants and gift shops located in Ohio and one in Sarasota, Florida. Three of those locations include lodging and one also has a theater.

240 US-20, Middlebury, 574-825-9471
essenhaus.com

With seating for 1,100, Das Dutchman Essenhaus is the largest restaurant in the state.

EL TACO REAL

Traditional Mexican from-scratch cuisine

For over 50 years, diners have been flocking to Hammond for the "real taco." Authentic traditional Mexican cuisine served up by friendly staff was the goal when Raymundo and Esther Garcia opened the doors of El Taco Real in 1974. The couple already had experience running the restaurant El Farolito in East Chicago in years prior.

They purchased a former Igloo ice cream shop on the 900 block of Hoffman Street that was expanded in later years with an additional dining room and bar.

The restaurant now continues under the helm of a second generation. Raymundo Garcia Jr. has been in the business since he was a teenager, and he's the face of the place. He is often greeting people at the door or chatting with longtime customers. He emphasizes how he wants people to feel like family when they are there, and his warm charm makes newcomers into regulars. It's cozy and warm, and with a margarita or two, it's like a fiesta with family.

The dishes are made in a traditional Mexican manner with a modern flair. Nothing is remade or reheated. Everything is fresh and made from scratch to order.

They offer three different options on carryout: "Eat now," "Eat later," and "Eat tomorrow." The first is fully assembled the way you'd get it if you dined in. If you want it later, you can get everything hot but packed separately to assemble at home. And the latter is a whole kit that's cold and just needs to be reheated before serving.

The menu runs the gamut from those items immediately recognized by Americans, like tacos, burritos, fajitas, and enchiladas, to the less familiar, like sopes, menudo, tortas, chili rellenos, huevos rancheros, and pazole.

Clockwise, from top left: Chips with fresh salsa and pico de gallo are brought to the table as an appetizer before your meal. Bring your appetite for generous entrée portions accompanied by rice and beans. A variety of authentic dishes are served at El Taco Real, including ones using their popular mole sauce. Be sure to try the guacamole, made fresh daily with avocado, onion, tomato, and a touch of spice.

A customer favorite and top seller is the Queso Fundido, especially the version topped with chorizo. You can also get your choice of their famous pork filling, chicken, or picadillo-style beef.

Passing on dessert just shouldn't be allowed here. With selections like the Fruit Finale house specialty (a puff pastry for two filled with cream cheese and slices of fresh fruit with strawberry sauce), flan, bunuelitos (crisp pastry sprinkled with cinnamon and sugar), rice pudding de leche, and cajeta crepes, savor that sweet taste of Mexico before you head out the door.

The house margaritas and daiquiris are pretty irresistible, but if you're a beer drinker, you'll also be pleased. You'll find several less common imports, like Pacifico, Tecate, Sol, Dos Equis Ambar, and Negra Modelo, as well as Dos Equis, Modelo, and some local craft brews on tap.

935 Hoffman St., Hammond, 219-932-8333
eltacorealrestaurant.com

Like it hot? Order it "Raymundo-style" for an extra kick.

TRIPLE XXX FAMILY RESTAURANT

Throwback diner has its own root beer brand

Since 1929, Triple XXX Family Restaurant has been a haven for locals, students at the nearby Purdue University Campus and road travelers looking for a hearty meal. Showcased on Food Network's *Diners, Drive-Ins and Dives*, the orange-and-black-clad eatery and its namesake root beer have amassed a number of accolades. Best Diner in Indiana by MSNBC. Top 50 Best Burgers list by *USA Today*. Most Iconic Soft Drink in Indiana by Thrillist. Those are a few.

The root beer itself predates the restaurant. Its production dates back to 1895. By the 1920s, there were close to 100 Triple XXX Thirst Stations around the country and in Canada with more than 150 bottlers producing it. Indiana is now the only remaining Triple XXX Family Restaurant location and the only one bottling and serving the beloved root beer.

When current owners Greg and Carrie Ehresman purchased the root beer brand, they made sure it was just like the original recipe. It's bottled in Chicago and distributed to retailers in Indiana and selected areas throughout the country as well as available at the restaurant. You can also purchase it online through the restaurant's website.

The menu has several sandwiches named for Purdue athletes, like the Duane Purvis All American quarter-pound chop steak with creamy peanut butter, American cheese, lettuce, tomato, pickle, and onion on a toasted sesame seed bun. The "chop steak" is a special 100 percent pure sirloin that is hand cut and ground in-house, and you can really taste the difference.

Left: With winding counter tops throughout the eatery, all the seats are stools. *Right:* The Duane Pervis All American Burger, a quarter pound chop steak patty with creamy peanut butter, American cheese, lettuce, tomato, pickle, and onion, was featured on the Food Network.

Much of what you'll taste is made from scratch the old-fashioned way, like the homemade potato salad and barbecue pork. Shakes are hand dipped using Blue Bell ice cream. The restaurant was way before its time with an open-concept kitchen before that became a thing, doing farm to fork since day one and crafting smash burgers long before the craze began.

Another thing that makes it such an appealing place is that you can get breakfast anytime. And the choices are scrumptious. Melt-in-your-mouth buttermilk biscuits. Chicken fried steak. Sausage gravy. Corned beef hash. Fluffy pancakes. Thick french toast. Cheesy omelets.

Whenever possible, the Ehresmans source locally and use Indiana products, like Red Gold. The sausage gravy is made with a course-ground proprietary whole hog blend made nearby by Beutler's Meats. A root beer jelly used in some of their dishes and sold at the restaurant is produced in Bremen.

The menu is constantly evolving and kept fresh with new recipes. A recent one is the "Ashely Burkhardt," named for the Purdue softball standout who went on to play professional softball and is now a coach, trainer, and podcast host. Chicken tenders are tossed in a sauce that uses their root beer jelly, barbecue sauce, and honey and is placed on grilled buttermilk biscuits. They also have a new root beer Bundt cake that is made from scratch in-house and served warm with ice cream.

The inside couldn't be more nostalgic and charming with a winding countertop that allows everyone to sit at the counter while they enjoy their meal. If you prefer to dine outdoors, you can do so year-round at one of their tent-enclosed tables.

2 N Salisbury St., West Lafayette, 765-743-5373
triplexxxfamilyrestaurant.com

THE RATHSKELLER

Indy's Germantown gem serves up authentic Bavarian cuisine

Part of the lifestyle of the Turner movement in the 19th century was the idea of obtaining a sound body and sound mind. The Turner movement was popular in German culture and was the main focus in the creation of Das Dutch House in Indianapolis. Built in the 1890s, it is one of the best-preserved structures dedicated to German American culture in the Midwest.

Now known as the Athenaeum, the building was created in German Renaissance Revival style and is listed three times on the National Register of Historic Places. Among its key features are copper-covered cupolas, stone lions, and arched and stained glass windows. One of the building's architects was the grandfather of author Kurt Vonnegut.

The Athenaeum is currently a multipurpose facility with a gymnasium and boutique YMCA, an auditorium, a coffee shop, gallery space, a biergarten, a 200-seat cabaret-style theater, and more. The bar area was once an open-air biergarten that was later enclosed.

An outdoor biergarten is now situated up the stairs and out the door. It's a bustling spot in the warmer months where live entertainment and festivals have guests raising their steins in the air and shouting "Prost!" It also offers a beautiful view of downtown Indy.

The restaurant, the Rathskeller, is situated on the lower level. Rathskeller is a German word that refers to a tavern that is in the basement or cellar of a public hall, and this one has been serving up Bavarian specialties since 1894, making it one of the oldest restaurants in the state. By square footage, it's the biggest restaurant in the city.

If you're looking for some authentic German cuisine, you'll be able to get your fill here. Whereas many eateries bring out a basket of bread

Left: Originally called Das Deutsche House, the Athenaeum is on the National Register of Historic Places. *Right:* A traditional weiner schnitzel is a popular menu item.

and butter at the start of your meal, the Rathskeller brings out a giant pretzel with beer cheese and spicy mustard for dipping. And be sure to start out slow on the mustard. It's got a fiery finish that will bring tears to your eyes.

Many of the German specialties are made from scratch, just like a German oma would make, among them sauerbraten (beef roast marinated for five days, slow-roasted, and topped with brown gravy accented with tones of currant and ginger); kassler ripchen (center-cut hardwood-smoked pork chop topped with a sauce of apples, golden raisins, walnuts, and herbs); and schnitzel (center-cut pork loin cutlet pan-fried in their house breading, topped with lemon slices and served with a lemon dipping sauce).

Sausages are made from traditional Bavarian recipes by a local German butcher shop, Claus' German Sausage & Meat, a family-run business that started in 2013. A hot wurst platte appetizer is presented with a sampling of bratwurst, bockwurst, keilbasse, and German wieners with homemade sauerkraut and red cabbage and mustards for dipping.

German imports, as well as other hard-to-find European beers, flow from the Rathskeller's tappers. They're one of the biggest-volume sellers of Warsteiner in the country.

401 E Michigan St., Indianapolis, 317-636-0396
rathskeller.com

The Athenaeum appeared in two big films. Interior shots in the movie *Eight Men Out* were filmed there, and some exterior shots in the movie *Going All the Way* were filmed in the biergarten.

MINER-DUNN

Home of the Old English cheeseburger and signature sherbet

There are a lot of places to get a cheeseburger, but only one place to get the unmistakable Miner-Dunn burger. It's been a favorite of locals for more than nine decades, drawing in customers with its high-quality, homemade menu items, nostalgic feel, and customer service.

Harold Miner and Ralph Dunn defied the odds by opening a restaurant during the Great Depression. The regional hamburger chain first opened in 1932 in Hammond. It was a modest location with just six stools and a small kitchen, and it quickly grew. There were once several locations in the Calumet region in both Indiana and Illinois. Today, only one remains.

The restaurant in Highland is the only place to go for that freshly made hamburger blend topped with creamy, sharp Old English cheese. It is best enjoyed with a pile of fresh-cut fries on the side or freshly-sliced battered onion rings. And when you order the deluxe meal, it comes with their signature orange sherbet that is made in-house.

Everything on the menu is made the old-fashioned way from scratch. Corned beef and roast beef are seasoned, trimmed, cooked, and sliced in-house for the Reuben and french dip sandwiches. Meat loaf is made from a longtime recipe. Scratch-made soups are made fresh each day. Homemade pie is the perfect finish to a meal. At least four varieties are available each day, and seasonal flavors like strawberry are extremely popular.

> **Be sure to try their special Old English cheese, a longtime staple that goes on their famous burgers and has a creamy sharpness to it.**

Left: The large vintage sign on Indianapolis Boulevard draws in customers to this fun nostalgic diner. *Top right:* The signature orange sherbet comes with your meal you order it "deluxe." *Bottom right:* Miner-Dunn has been doing smash burger type sandwiches for decades—long before they became popular. Thin patties are served on buns with fresh-cut fries.

Walking in the door is like a trip back in time to an era when teenagers sat at counters in poodle skirts sipping on creamy hand-dipped shakes. The neon sign outside lures diners in where they can find a seat on a stool or in a booth and bite into a taste of nostalgia.

The current owner is Joe Samara, who has owned the place for decades and is the second owner. He attributes their ongoing success to the multiple generations who have become regulars. Grandparents bring their grandkids here to enjoy a meal that they enjoyed growing up—and as long as that continues, they'll still keep doing things the old-fashioned way.

8940 Indianapolis Blvd., Highland, 219-923-3311
minerdunnhamburgers.com

VALPO VELVET

Four generations of creating dreamy ice cream

In 1947, Herb Brown realized his goal of having his own dairy business. He purchased the Valparaiso Home Ice Company, which delivered ice, ice cream, and other dairy products in the area, and it became Brown's Dairy.

A graduate of the University of Wisconsin, Brown earned a degree in dairy science and became production manager of Goldenrod Ice Cream Company and then Central Ice Cream Company in Chicago after graduating.

When he read in the *Chicago Tribune* that Valparaiso Home Ice Company was for sale, he saw it as an opportunity to make his dream come true, and he was soon producing his own Valpo Velvet Ice Cream.

His son, Gordon, joined the business after also graduating from the University of Wisconsin in dairy science. He introduced a cottage cheese to the dairy line that was very popular. When Herb retired in 1971, he sold the business to Gordon and the tradition continued. Gordon opted to transition away from the milk delivery business but decided to keep making ice cream.

In 1974, Gordon remodeled the old milk production plant and converted it into an ice cream parlor and family restaurant while continuing to produce Valpo Velvet ice cream. After he passed away in 1995, his sons, Mike and Mark, remodeled the restaurant and decided to reopen it as a sandwich shop and ice cream parlor. Today, more than 75 years after Brown Dairy began, a fourth generation is behind the counter carrying on their great-grandfather's legacy.

Valpo Velvet got a fresh look in 2023 and dropped the sandwich shop part of the business. You can still go in and enjoy a number of frosty treats in their dining room or on their outdoor patio.

They make a total of about 60 flavors of ice cream, sherbet, sorbet,

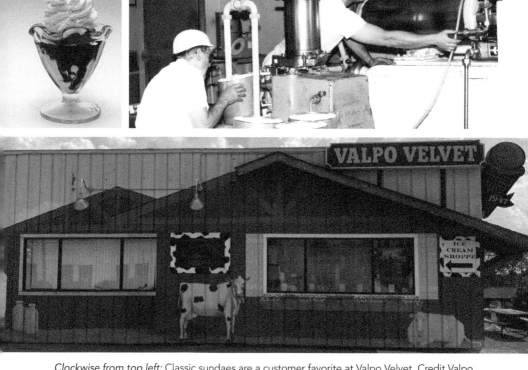

Clockwise from top left: Classic sundaes are a customer favorite at Valpo Velvet. Credit Valpo Velvet. Gordon Brown and son, Mike, working in the ice cream production facility. Credit Valpo Velvet. The exterior of Valpo Velvet has changed over the years, but there are always bright inviting colors gracing the facade.

and frozen yogurt and also offer a gluten-free ice cream. Customer favorites include mint chocolate chip, butter pecan, and cookies and cream. You'll find all the classic flavors here as well as some decadent concoctions like butterscotch ripple, cheery cheesecake, black walnut, black raspberry chip, Aztec hot chocolate, cinnamon spice, chocolate-dipped strawberry, rum raisin, and green tea.

The ice cream has developed a reputation of being extremely high quality using locally sourced products when available and is distributed to wholesale locations in Indiana and Illinois. You'll find it in more than 50 retail sites, and it is served at more than a dozen restaurants. Valpo Velvet also has trucks that make their way out to local events to scoop up treats and can be rented for private events.

57 Monroe St., Valparaiso, 219-464-4141
valpovelvet.com

MAYBERRY CAFE

Where *The Andy Griffith Show* plays on repeat with an Aunt Bee–approved menu

Even at the time it aired, *The Andy Griffith Show* harkened back to simpler days in small-town America—and one in which any problem could be solved in the sitcom's half-hour slot. Andy Griffith continues to charm audiences with a dose of nostalgia and a cast of characters that you couldn't help but love in the fictional town of Mayberry.

The show retains such a following that the town of Danville, Indiana, has a café dedicated solely to the beloved show. Mayberry Cafe opened in 1992 in the downtown square. It's a charming little Mayberry-esque place, and the café fits in perfectly. It's located on a corner on the square across from the Hendricks County Courthouse, where a 1962 Ford Galaxy sheriff's car painted to resemble the TV version sits parked outside.

Inside, you'll feel like you're in your grandma's country kitchen with flowery wallpaper, checker-backed booths, and wood tables like the ones you'd eat a big Sunday supper at when you're at home. The walls are lined with photos of the cast and framed scenes of memorable episodes. A couple television screens have *The Andy Griffith Show* playing nonstop episodes on a loop.

The menu is filled with items featuring character names, going along with the theme of the show—all foods that you might expect to find on Aunt Bee's table. Aunt Bee's Fried Pickles. Opie's Prize Catch Blue Gill. Myer's Lake Special Catfish. Barney's Burger. The Andy's Tenderloin is described as a "sheriff-size hand cut pork tenderloin." There's a list of "Barney's Side Car" items that go great with all of the country-inspired entrées: mashed potatoes, green beans, cinnamon apples, mac-n-cheese, sweet potato fries, and more.

Left: Fried biscuits may be on the appetizer menu, but they're sweet and scrumptious and could serve as dessert as well. They are served warm along with apple butter. You can enjoy them while watching episodes of *The Andy Griffith Show*, which are shown on televisions while you dine. *Center:* You can expect a hearty home cooked meal just like Aunt Bee would have served to Andy and Opie when you dine at Mayberry Cafe. *Right:* The cafe sits on the square across from the county courthouse.

Some of the most popular items are the homemade meat loaf, the smothered chopped steak, and Aunt Bee's Fried Chicken. Wash it all down with a glass of huckleberry lemonade (which you can also buy by the gallon).

Save room for a sweet treat. Desserts include mug cakes—Ernest T's Mountain Dew Mug Cake and Aunt Bee's Chocolate Mug Cake—and several pies, crisps and cobblers. You can also enjoy a simple Opie's Sundae of ice cream with syrup, whipped cream, and sprinkles, the Apple Pie Supreme or Monkey on Your Back brownie topped with vanilla ice cream and chocolate syrup drizzle.

Be sure to take home a souvenir on your way out. There's a variety of Mayberry Cafe T-shirts, mugs, and an Aunt Bee's Mayberry Cookbook.

The place has received lots of attention, and numerous newspaper clippings of the restaurant's success hang in the lobby. The town even hosted a Mayberry Festival for several years that drew fans of the show from all over.

78 W Main St., Danville, 317-745-4067
mayberrycafe.com

HOSTESS HOUSE

Wealthy businessman's gift to wife
now elegant restaurant

Dating back to 1912, the Hostess House is one of the most opulent homes in Marion. J. Wood Wilson, a prominent businessman, had it built as a wedding gift for his bride, Peggy Pampai, who was 33 years younger than him.

The mansion was designed by Samuel Plato, one of the first Black architectural designers and building contractors. Plato was born in 1881 in Alabama in a slave cabin and learned construction from his father, attended the State University of Louisville, and then enrolled in the International Correspondence School in Pennsylvania, where he received his formal architectural training. Over the course of his career he built about 40 different post office buildings and was awarded several defense housing contracts at a time when it was rare for Blacks to receive government contracts.

The home had been abandoned when Wilson's widow moved to New York. She had returned to the home and briefly lived there with her second husband, Dr. John-Colin Vaughn.

Later a group of socialites in the Marion community started an effort to renovate the structure to be used as a center of entertainment where they could host guests outside of their homes.

Now known as the Wilson-Vaughan Hostess House, the mansion is used as a public event space, hosting weddings, cultural events, and social gatherings. There is also a restaurant inside that operates for lunch on weekdays from 11 a.m. to 2 p.m. in one of the mansion's impressive dining rooms, and a boutique is situated on the second floor.

Clockwise, from left: The Hostess House offers a luxurious atmosphere with a casual lunch menu in a historic mansion. A marker in front of the home highlights the contribution of one of the country's early Black architects in the design of the mansion. The lavishly appointed dining rooms in the restaurant provide a bit of nostalgia. A variety of sandwiches are served, like the classic Reuben. A signature dessert served at Hostess House is the decadent butterscotch pie.

The home has beautiful, detailed woodwork, glasswork, fireplaces, drapery, and other decorative touches. Enjoying a meal there transports you to a slower time of elegance and opulence.

With the restaurant menu available only for lunchtime, it consists of mainly sandwiches and salads along with a soup of the day. Highlights include a pecan chicken salad, a harvest spinach salad, a classic Reuben, a pork tenderloin sandwich, and a cranberry turkey sandwich.

Finish off your meal with their signature apple dumplings and butterscotch pie. It's worth the trip just for a peek at the interior of the home and a piece of the pie.

723 W 4th St., Marion, 765-664-3755
hostesshouse.org

CATELLO'S ITALIAN ART CUISINE

A small-town gem with authentic Southern Italian cuisine

Nestled in the charming downtown of Pendleton is a little corner building with a restaurant and deli that take you far away to a kitchen in Naples. Catello Avagnale came to the United States to open a restaurant after his longtime friend, who had also opened an Italian restaurant in Indiana, Matteo's Ristorante Italiano in Noblesville, urged him to do the same. In 2016, this chef-owned eatery came to be, and as the name suggests, the food is nothing short of art.

The son of a cheesemaker, Avagnale brought this skill with him and prepares his own mozzarella and burrata in-house. It's a feast for the eyes and paradise for the taste buds. It's the perfect start to your culinary tour of Italy and, of course, it's not the only thing made from scratch. Everything, as a matter of fact, is made from scratch. The sauces, the cheeses, the breads, the pastas.

The old-world ambiance is inviting and cozy, and Catello's passion makes the meal there just that much more meaningful. He's a visible presence in the dining room, where beyond greeting and chatting with customers, he can be found table-side putting on a show as he ignites a shot of bourbon and then weaves his freshly made pasta into a slowly melting wheel of cheese. This is one of those experiences that make the eatery a destination that people will travel an hour or more for. If you hear someone say that it is the best Italian restaurant in Indiana, you can believe them.

Left: A tableside pasta wheel preparation will wow guests at Catello's Italian Art Cuisine. *Center:* Freshly made cheeses are a unique feature of dining at Catello's. *Top right:* Homemade layered lasagna that melts in your mouth is covered with a housemate sauce. *Bottom right:* Desserts are made from scratch, including cakes, gelato, and tiramisu, pictured here.

Next to the dining room is the INItaly Deli and Gelato Shop, where you can buy imported products as well as wines, freshly made meals, pasta, sauces, and desserts.

The lunchtime menu has some more casual panini and pizza selections along with pastas and entrées. A new, separate, nearby eatery is in the planning stages where pizza pies will be the focus.

You taste the freshness in every bite, starting with appetizers like fried calamari and shrimp (frittura di peace), meatballs with bolognese sauce (polpette and bolognese), bruschetta, and fresh-sliced cheese and meat platters. The menu items are listed by their Italian names, but with an English translation below. Several different pasta varieties can be found on the menu, from rigatoni to fettuccine to pappardelle to stuffed ravioli and tortellini, along with a lovely layered lasagna bolognese.

Desserts are made with just as much love as everything else on the menu. You can't go wrong with anything. The selection of cakes includes a scrumptious coconut apricot cake and a lemon blackberry cheesecake that you won't find anywhere else. Traditional tiramisu, cannoli, and crème brûlée round out the finishing options.

103 E State St., Pendleton, 765-221-9052
catellos.com

BLUEBEARD

Award-winning chefs and farmer partnerships make it a must-go

If trendy dining is your thing, there's no better spot to be than Bluebeard in Indianapolis. This award-winning restaurant in the Fletcher Place neighborhood sits in a renovated 1924 warehouse serving up phenomenal shared plates and craft cocktails.

Bluebeard has been a standout since opening in 2012, boasting one of the best chefs in the Midwest for many years of its operation. Everything on the menu is made from scratch utilizing fresh, seasonal, and often local ingredients through farmer partnerships. It means that quality is consistent and the menu changes to meet the point of optimum harvest.

All of the bread served at Bluebeard is made at their in-house bakery called Amelia's. There's a separate entrance for the bakery, so you can stop in to shop for some amazing baked goods even if you're not staying to dine. Every morning at 4 a.m. the ovens warm to fill with hundreds of loaves of fresh breads, pastries, cookies, and other treats. They're now served in restaurants all over the city, too.

The bakery actually preceded the restaurant. With no place to buy hearth-made European-style bread in the area, Tom Battista wanted to change that. When he found the former factory where the bakery would be housed, it had more room than needed and the idea for Bluebeard was born.

Wine is curated by the house sommelier with thoughtfully crafted cocktails made from fine spirits and house-made sodas and syrups. In addition to the main dining room and bar area, the Rosewater Room,

Left: Flavored butters and spreads with freshly toasted bread is one of the appetizers that has been featured at Bluebeard. *Center:* A portrait of Indianapolis native Kurt Vonnegut hangs in the restaurant, which shares a name with one of his novels. *Right:* The menu at Bluebeard is full of seasonal specialties that utilize the current harvest.

which is steeped in 19th-century charm, can accommodate up to 40 guests. A second-story space also has an open kitchen and space for up to 18 guests.

The menu is innovative and creative and has earned its chefs the distinction of being James Beard finalists. Former executive chef Abbi Merriss was a six-time James Beard Foundation Award semifinalist. Her successor, Alan Sternberg, had also been a James Beard Foundation finalist in his earlier roles.

The name of the eatery was inspired by one of Indy's best-known sons, Kurt Vonnegut. Bluebeard was one of the 14 novels he wrote in his controversial half-century career as a writer. Hints and nods to Vonnegut are all around the interior of the restaurant, as well.

The restaurant doesn't take reservations, but it's worth the wait if there happens to be one. In between lunch and dinner service is a "snack menu" served from 3 p.m. to 5 p.m.

653 Virginia Ave., Indianapolis, 317-686-1580
bluebeardindy.com

OLD COLONIAL INN

Fine dining in a former hotel

Built in 1894, Hotel Kentland has been a longtime landmark with a decorative tower set above the two-story brick building on the courthouse square in Newton County. The hotel remained in operation until the 1960s, and in 1964, it opened as the Old Colonial Inn Restaurant.

Just over a decade ago, the current owners, Mike and Mara Davis, took over and the place underwent an extensive restoration. They opened the fine-dining establishment in 2014, and each year on their anniversary they share a social media post with the totals of what they've served so far. The most recent post revealed that they'd served 58,930 dinners, 24,240 baked potatoes, 35,807 salads, 13,224 desserts, and 18,312 glasses of wine since their opening.

The downtown square is a little different than most as it has been updated with a center parking lane that splits the road that the restaurant is situated on. The side of the street where the restaurant is has a definite vintage feel. You can walk under the overhang of the building almost picturing a wooden sidewalk below and a horse tied up to an outer post. The brick, woodwork, and sign all point to the past, but the place has been well maintained and beautifully restored.

Inside, you feel the elegance of the era with white tablecloths, dim lighting, and very high-quality ingredients. Hanging on the walls are old photos that harken back to a different time and newspaper clippings of the building's former hotel days.

Start off with a classic cocktail or glass of wine from their collection. The old fashioned is something you'll definitely want to try as it has a touch that makes it quite unique. The Maker's Mark that is used in the drink is aged on-site for three weeks. It is first chilled in fruit for the first 24 hours and then transferred to wood barrels for another 21 days.

Old Colonial Inn

Top: Set in an 1894 former hotel building, the vintage-looking Old Colonial Inn sign hangs in front of the entrance. *Bottom left:* Fried shrimp with cocktail sauce is an option on the appetizer menu. *Bottom right: High-quality* steaks rival those of the state's high-end steakhouses.

The menu has all the marks of a classic American steak house. Shrimp cocktail as an appetizer. A basket of bread and butter. A soup or salad before the entrée. And a number of select cuts of fine steaks, seafood, and more.

Roast prime rib of beef is front and center on the menu and comes in English or regular cut with a New York strip and filet mignon as additional beef choices. Salmon, shrimp, pike, perch, and lobster tail are among the seafood choices. A couple of pasta dishes, a pork shank, and a chicken breast round out the menu, which is brief, but covers all the fine-dining bases. You can expect superior-quality meats and seafood prepared to your specifications.

Don't even think about skipping dessert! The tuxedo cake, a layered chocolate cake with a whipped vanilla filling and fudgy icing, is divine.

216 N 3rd St., Kentland, 219-474-6774
oldcolonialinn.com

PAYNE'S RESTAURANT

Get authentic fish and chips at this British-themed establishment

Set a little off the road, it's worth seeking out Payne's. Once you get closer, a tall sign is likely to capture your attention. It's in the color and similar design of the Union Jack, the flag of the United Kingdom. Atop it is an arrow signaling you to this spot where you may find yourself speaking with a hint of a British accent when you make your way out the door.

Outside you'll also find a statue of Garfield, the big orange cat, dressed as a British soldier. His presence may seem odd until you learn that his creator, Jim Davis, was from the area and the Grant County Tourism office is promoting a Garfield Trail with more than a dozen statues of the cat around the county in garb related to the spot where he was placed.

You're greeted with the obligatory "Keep Calm and Carry On" sign and more touches of England in the decor. Once inside, it's a casual and cozy pub filled with wooden chairs and booths with decoupage tabletops. Another room gives groovy 1960s vibes with its wood-paneled ceiling and large macramé chandeliers.

Whereas complimentary bread is often served at the start of a meal or chips and salsa in a Mexican establishment, Payne's offers up a plate of freshly made black bean dip along with tortilla or corn chips to munch on while you wait for your entrée.

The menu is inspired by cuisine from the home county of owner Stephen Payne, who was born in Yorkshire, England. It started as Payne's Custard and Coffee and has evolved to the full-service restaurant and pub that it is today as an eclectic and charismatic venue in which to relax and socialize.

Left: Classic fish and chips—complete with a mini British flag—are a must when dining at Payne's. *Center:* A "Keep Calm and Carry On" sign greets diners as they enter the British-themed eatery. *Right:* Unique macramé lighting fixtures grace the dining room

Hand-battered and deep-fried cod in a traditional British crispy batter with fries, tartar sauce, and malt vinegar—aka fish 'n chips—is the star of the menu for sure, but there are other British specialties that just need to be tried as well, including bangers and mash, British chicken curry, and beef stew and Yorkshire pudding. The mashed potatoes served alongside the bangers are made with a rutabaga and potato blend with a sweet apple cider and onion gravy.

And about the soup du jour. There are several different varieties that you won't find in your average American restaurant that you'll want to sample, like cock-a-leekie soup made with leeks, prunes, and chicken or black bean and tomato soup.

Sticky toffee pudding, rhubarb crumble, and bread pudding à la mode are worth abandoning your diet for.

They've added a vegan dahl and vegetarian eggplant to cater to varying dietary needs in addition to making a lot of the food gluten free or gluten free modifiable. In warmer months, you'll find the Payne's food truck at events all over the state of Indiana serving up their delicious British grub.

4925 S Kay Bee Dr., Gas City, 765-998-0668
places.singleplatform.com/paynes-custard-and-coffe-shop/menu

SHAPIRO'S DELICATESSEN

Traditional Jewish deli and bakery is oldest single-family deli in country

Way back in 1905, Shapiro's Grocery Deli opened in the working-class neighborhood just south of downtown Indianapolis. Louis and Rebecca Shapiro had arrived a couple years earlier after fleeing their homeland in Ukraine where their family had been in the delicatessen business since 1795.

They first sold dry goods on the street from a pushcart (Indy's first food truck!) before opening the brick-and-mortar business where they lived above the store with their eight children. Three of their sons took over the business in the 1930s, and following Prohibition, they started selling beer along with salami and corned beef sandwiches. They also added tables and chairs and began serving dinner entrées, like their mother's spaghetti and meatballs recipe, in a cafeteria-style dining room.

Son Max Shapiro kept the business running into his 80s, spending 65 years in the family business. His nephew and grand-nephew took over following his death, and today, the great-grandson of Louis and Rebecca, Brian Shapiro, is at the helm with his wife, Sally. It remains the oldest single-family deli in America.

Over the years, they expanded the location to add a full bakery. Today, the longtime traditions continue of using high-quality ingredients in cherished family recipes with quick and friendly service.

The place is bustling pretty much any time of day.

Corned beef hash, omelets, and lox and bagels will get your day started off right. Sandwiches play a starring role in the menu, with the corned beef sandwich having been named "the finest corned beef sandwich in the world" by *USA Today*. It is a brined and seasoned quality cut that is shaved when hot.

Left: Hearty comfort classics like stew have been longtime staples of the deli. *Center:* Sally Shapiro and her husband, Brian, now run the restaurant, which was started by the great-grandson of the founders. *Right:* A variety of sandwiches, sides and entrées can be found on the menu at Shapiro's.

Beyond that, you can get their equally loved pastrami, rare roast beef, and brisket sandwiches that are hand-trimmed and sliced and served on their own homemade breads and buns. The hand-sliced rye bread is a game changer and will make you never want thin machine-sliced bread again. Chopped liver, salami, smoked tongue, Alaskan pollack, chicken salad, and albacore tuna are some of the additional sandwich options.

Everything made at Shapiro's is fresh, like the five soup varieties they have every day (yes, one is matzo ball). Potatoes are peeled. Fresh cabbage is chopped. Whole chickens are cooked. And you'll taste the difference.

For dinner, you'll find every comfort food imaginable: meat loaf, baked chicken, stuffed cabbage, roast beef, beef stew, stuffed peppers, spaghetti, short ribs, and more.

On the bakery side, everything is made on-site from scratch—from pies to pastries to cookies to cannoli. There are also several flavors of rugelach, a traditional filled Jewish baked confection.

808 S Meridian St., Indianapolis, 317-631-4041
shapiros.com

You'll also find a Shapiro's Delicatessen counter at the Indianapolis Airport.

ROOT & BONE

A Southern revival of farm and garden to table

This isn't the place to go if you're into exclusive, haughty, pretentious establishments with bite-sized portions. This is the place to go if you love an elevated plate of good down-home, stick-to-your-ribs, made-with-love grub that's better than Grandma used to make (sorry, Granny!). While there are some lighter menu items to choose from, it's best to just shut your eyes to calorie count, wear your stretchy pants, and savor every delicious, deep-fried bite.

They describe the place as having "honest southern food, soul-nurturing, conscientiously sourced, farm-fresh ingredients. A craftsman's ethic coupled with artistic culinary thought. A tribute to the timeless recipes and traditions of a rural America and the warm embrace of its hospitality."

The chefs behind this culinary mastery are Janine Booth and Jeff McInnis. Booth was born and raised in Australia and made her way to Miami in 2010. In 2013 she was scouted for Bravo's Emmy Award–winning television show *Top Chef*, where she competed against 18 contestants in New Orleans.

McInnis, a Florida native, appeared on *Top Chef* in 2008, then set his roots in Miami, where he earned a place as a James Beard semifinalist at Yardbird Southern Table. The couple opened the first location of Root & Bone in New York in 2013. It was an instant hit, earning several awards right out of the gate, including "Best Fried Chicken in New York City" from multiple publications.

Root & Bone opened in Indianapolis in early 2020 with owner-partners the Luke Family of Brands and IndyCar driver James Hindcliffe. It's housed in a 1927 building of Indiana limestone in Indy's Broad Ripple neighborhood.

Left: Corn soufflé is a southern side that pairs well with the entrées at Root and Bone. *Center:* An ideal spot for brunch, pair a mimosa with some chicken biscuits. *Right:* The short rib meat loaf is a signature item that is a must try.

In true Southern style, there is not a dinner menu but a "supper" menu. There are too many highlights to list, but a visit would not be complete without trying the r&b chicken biscuits made with Grandma Daisy's angel biscuits, signature fried chicken filets, and Tabasco pepper jelly with pickles. The biscuits are amazing on their own, but next level when paired with their scrumptious signature chicken, which is brined in sweet tea.

Low-country shrimp cocktail, drunken deviled eggs, and fried green tomatoes are among the other popular starters.

The salads feature the freshest of the seasonal offerings, and there's nothing like the peach salad with burrata, grilled peaches, shaved fennel, arugula, and corn bread croutons.

Aside from their award-winning fried chicken, one other dish that you simply cannot skip is the short rib meat loaf. The braised short ribs are shredded with caramelized onions and then formed into a loaf that sits for a full day before being seared in a cast-iron pan. Placed next to a pile of creamy mashed potatoes and gravy, it's pure heaven on a plate.

With the eclectic, hospitable vibe and lineup of indulgent Southern dishes, it's a great place to enjoy brunch along with some fabulous signature cocktails.

There are now two locations in the Hoosier State after another location opened in Chesterton at the end of 2023.

4601 N College Ave., Indianapolis, 317-602-8672
rootnboneindy.com

ALBANO'S

Stuffed pasta like no other

Nobody makes pasta like Nick Albano. Some call him the "Pasta Daddy." His fans are sometimes called "pastatutes." He comes from a long line of good Italian cooks, and pasta is just in his Italian genes. His first restaurant was in the Duneland town of Chesterton and he then worked out of a number of spaces in Valparaiso before returning to where he started. He's also been a popular vendor at farmer's markets locally and in Chicago and at other public events, where he prepares servings of pasta with homemade sauces right before your eyes, the smell of garlic wafting around the radius as he works his magic.

Tortellini and ravioli are his specialties, and the varieties ebb and flow with the season. He sources many ingredients locally, stuffing each piece with freshly made morsels of high-quality vegetables, herbs, and meats.

You'll want to start out your meal with Daddy's Super Delicious Bread, a freshly made artisan bread accompanied with fennel pollen olive oil and a slow-simmered 12-hour red sauce.

Salads are loaded with fresh, local ingredients, like the spring salad of shaved brussels sprouts, charred cauliflower, roasted gourmet mushrooms, and pecorino tossed in house-made lemon vinaigrette.

The starter you simply cannot miss is Mommy Mom's Meatballs made with grass-fed beef and basil in a generous pool of eight-hour red sauce and topped with house-made ricotta and arugula. You can also enjoy the meatballs in an order of hand-cut spaghetti and meatballs.

When it comes to the stuffed pasta, the scrumptious options make it almost too hard to choose. A hearty short rib tortellini is made with 12-hour braised short rib. A chicken tortellini is tossed in a delectable reduced garlic cream sauce with roasted local mushroom

Left: Homemade cheesecake offerings are all handmade from family recipes. Pictured is the honey lavender cheesecake. *Right:* Stuffed tortellini is the specialty at Albano's, with varieties that rotate seasonally.

and asparagus. There's even a rabbit tortellini of rabbit confit in a spicy cacciatore sauce. A rich lobster tortellini will exceed your expectations.

Even if you're not vegetarian, you'll want to give every one of the veggie-stuffed pastas a try. Depending on the season, you'll find such varieties as sweet potato ravioli, potato chive tortellini, corn tortellini, caramelized onion tortellini, pumpkin and sage tortellini, tomato basil tortellini, sugar snap pea tortellini, and others.

Both a traditional Grammy's Lasagna and a mushroom lasagna are also on the menu.

A popular non-pasta entrée is a Faroe Island Salmon seared with a crispy skin and seasonal vegetables.

There's one dessert available—Mommy Mom's Cheesecake—but it comes in several flavors. They're all spectacular, but the honey lavender will leave you in awe and dreaming about it for weeks to come.

119 S Calumet Rd., Chesterton, 219-242-9160
eatalbanos.square.site

Nick Albano's pastas are highly sought after, and he was recruited to supply them to some other restaurants out of state that he's not able to divulge.

IVANHOE'S

Where you can get 100 different ice cream treats

There are few foods that conjure up as many cherished childhood memories as ice cream. And as grown-ups, we still scream for it.

Wiley's Drive-In was once a little walk-up sandwich stop where you ate your food at picnic tables, but in 1965, Ivan and Carol Slain bought the spot and Ivanhoe's Ice Cream and Sandwich Shop was born.

The name Ivanhoe came about when a teenage employee had been reading the historical novel of that title by Sir Walter Scott and called Ivan by that name. It stuck.

Burgers are made from fresh ground-round steak, sauce for their coney dogs is made fresh in-house every day, pulled pork is slow simmered in sauce, and the pork tenderloin is hand breaded. Homemade chicken salad is served over a freshly sliced fruit salad. There are also 10 different salads if you want to balance things out nicely and have veggies for a meal to counteract the sugary dessert.

But in this case, the sandwiches are really secondary. The majority of customers who come in are there for the ice cream. At Ivanhoe's, you can choose from 100 different shakes and 100 different sundaes. Each shake and sundae is assigned a number.

Some of the more unique sundaes are Banana Blue, a soft vanilla ice cream with bananas and blueberries; Bear Paw with hand-dipped chocolate ice cream, pretzels, and hot fudge; Cloud with soft vanilla ice cream and marshmallow topping, whipped cream, and coconut; Touchdown with hand-dipped peppermint ice cream, Mounds bar, and hot fudge; Trojan 1, hand-dipped mint chocolate chip ice cream with chocolate-covered graham crackers and hot fudge; and White Elephant with soft-serve vanilla ice cream, pretzels, cashews, and marshmallow topping.

Left: The name Ivanhoe was a nickname given to owner Ivan Slain after his teenage employee had been reading the historical novel of that name by Sir Walter Scott. *Center:* Ivanhoe's is in Grant County where you can follow the Garfield trail to see statues of this beloved cartoon cat created by local artist Jim Davis. At this stop the orange cat holds an ice cream cone. *Right:* Ice cream has the leading role here, where they have 100 different shakes and sundaes on the menu.

As for shakes, if you're looking for something different you may wish to indulge in the Aloha, a pineapple shake with bananas, coconut, and pecans topped with whipped cream and a cherry; Coffee Break with hand-dipped coffee ice cream with Chips Ahoy cookies; High Noon, made with hand-dipped orange sherbet mixed with vanilla soft-serve ice cream topped with a dip of french vanilla ice cream, pineapple topping, and a cherry; Krispy Kritter, cherry shake with chocolate chips and Krispies; or Shipwreck, a blueberry shake with pretzels poured over a dip of cookies.

Among the customer favorites are the mint chocolate chip shake and the turtle sundae.

There's one non–ice cream dessert that people clamor for all winter until it's back for the season again. The strawberry shortcake is highly anticipated and draws in huge crowds when it returns in the spring.

979 S Main St., Upland, 765-998-7261
ivanhoes.info

Regulars can track the ice cream treats they try on a card, and when they get through all 100, they get a special "100 Club" shirt and their name on the Wall of Fame.

49

TIPPECANOE PLACE

Fine dining in the former Studebaker Mansion

Sometimes you eat at a place where the food is wonderful, but the ambiance doesn't match. Or you eat in a stunning place where the food is lackluster. At Tippecanoe Place, you get the best of both worlds—impressive fine-dining fare in a stunning 19th-century mansion. Oh, and there is the bonus of a craft brewery on-site, as well.

The mansion was built for Clem Studebaker, who was president of the Studebaker Corporation, which was based in South Bend. Studebaker was founded in 1852 as a wagon manufacturer and moved into building automobiles, first with electric vehicles in 1902 and then gasoline vehicles in 1904. It was one of the most influential automakers of the 20th century.

Designed by Chicago architect Henry Ives Cobb, construction began on the Studebaker Mansion in 1886, and it was completed in 1889 for a cost of $250,000. Cobb was also designer of the Potter Palmer Mansion on Lake Shore Drive in Chicago. The 24,000-square-foot Studebaker Mansion has about 40 rooms. It's been a grand place for guests since the first ones were welcomed to the mansion in the late 1800s.

Every inch of the place oozes wealth and luxury, both inside and out on all four floors. The entrance to the restaurant leads you into a grand hall with a massive hand-carved staircase and a grand piano.

Today, diners enjoy grand cuisine inside the walls of a former library with a wide array of distinct wines. All the major players of fine dining are there: steaks, duck, rack of lamb, prime rib, seafood, pasta, and more.

Studebaker Brewing Company is situated on the second floor, and it offers a more casual vibe that is still within the elegant, historic spaces of the mansion. The brewery focuses on artisan ales and lagers

Clockwise, from left: Prime rib is one of the specialties offered in the dining room. Guests enter the restaurant through a set of original heavy wooden doors. As you enter the restaurant, you are greeted with a piano and grand staircase. The beautiful Studebaker Mansion, completed in 1889, now serves as a restaurant and craft brewery.

that are brewed on-site along with wines and specialty handcrafted classic cocktails. There's a casual menu of flatbreads, appetizers, and sandwiches. Start with some N'awlins Creole Shrimp or beer cheese and pretzel sticks, followed by a mac and cheese, prime rib sandwich, smoked barbecue brisket, or margherita flatbread.

If you're looking for a spot for an elegant Sunday brunch, this is your place. Choose from a nice selection of elevated entrées from 10 a.m. to 2 p.m.

The brewery is also a sponsor of the South Bend Cubs, and you can park there for free, stop in for a pregame drink, and walk over to the stadium.

620 W Washington St., South Bend, 574-234-9077
tippe.com

See an amazing collection of Studebaker automobiles at the nearby Studebaker Museum.

THE HULMAN

Boutique hotel's posh eatery
honors Indy Motor Speedway

On the corner of the lower level of Hotel Indy is a restaurant that hints to Indy's association with, and long history in, racing. Named for former Indianapolis Motor Speedway owner Tony Hulman, it has a subtle racing theme with an atmosphere that is warm and sleek and retro. It's one of a few local touches that bring the glory of this wonderful Midwest city to guests at the hotel.

The building, which is a Tribute Portfolio property, dates back to 1969 when it opened as a bank. It later served as law offices. After two years of renovations, it opened as Hotel Indy in October 2001. The decor and vibe throughout are reminiscent of its early era. As you walk through a groovy keyhole doorway entrance from the hotel to the dining room, it kind of makes you feel like you're on the set of a James Bond movie.

The building is an example of brutalist architecture with 3-foot concrete waffle ceilings between each floor that add an artsy flair and create a noise barrier.

During the renovations, an extra floor was added to the then five-floor structure that created a rooftop bar and lounge. It's a nice spot to sit back and soak in the city with a cocktail or pamper yourself with a Sunday brunch. It has seating for 30 outside and 60 inside and a dedicated express elevator to the top called the Cannonball Express. Cannonball was the nickname of Erwin Baker, the first winner of a

> A giant globe over the hotel bar was once on display in a local variety store on what was called the Brandon Block.

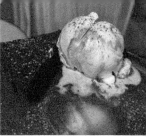

Left to right: Pork belly bites are a flavorful shareable item. A classic steak frites is one of the upscale entrée options. Desserts are decadent works of art that you won't want to pass up.

motorized race at the Indianapolis Motor Speedway, who won that first race on a motorcycle.

Hulman became the face of the speedway with his recognizable voice booming the famous words "Gentlemen, start your engines!" on race day. A private dining room in the restaurant is named the 1945, honoring the year that it was purchased. To get to the room, you step over a little black-and-white strip of tile signifying the trademark speedway flag.

Hotel restaurants are often the places where you can really see chefs shine, as they often have a good amount of creative control over the menu. Chef Danny Kener has brought in dishes that have a strong Midwest feel, but in elevated ways. His meaty, hearty short rib dish takes the traditional meat-and-potatoes standard and brings in that Indiana representation with the addition of polenta, since the state is known for its abundance of sweet corn.

A mushroom bolognese is one that was inspired by Italian traditions of slow and careful preparation. It takes four hours to cook using techniques not normally used in the industry anymore due to time and labor constraints.

Some simpler items are taken to new levels. An appetizer of bacon is made richer with confit preparation. Burrata is garnished with squash, pesto pomegranate, and pepitas. The burger is made of double layers of Wagyu beef with bacon jam and garlic aioli. Foods that may be ordinary are made extraordinary.

141 E Washington St., Indianapolis, 317-735-2527
hotelindy.com

MERRILLVILLE TEA ROOM

Adorable tearoom is connected to flower shop

Tea and florals are a winning combination. You'll find both under one roof at the Merrillville Florist & Tea Room. The longtime establishment closed briefly and then reopened in 2019 with new ownership.

You enter through the florist and gift shop, where you can get lovely arrangements, find some new teas to try, or pick up some decadent truffles or gift items. The tearoom winds through the long building with little intimate nooks for two and larger rooms for groups of varying sizes: the Red Velvet Room, French Door Room, Fireside Porch, and main dining room. It is a charming spot for any kind of celebration or special occasion.

Dining in the tearoom is a calming experience that takes you away from the hustle and bustle of our busy world and allows you to slow down and sip surrounded by beautiful decor and accents. It's also a nice spot for all ages, where you can connect with girlfriends or family, have a relaxing lunch date, or bring a little girl and spoil her as a princess for a day.

While the tearoom doesn't bring out your meal on the traditional afternoon tea tiered tray, you'll find some British-inspired items on the menu. The house specialty is the Chateau Earl Grey, made with chunks of chicken breast, broccoli, and cheese wrapped in a phyllo purse and drizzled with their house champagne sauce and a side of cranberry relish. Another is the Kingfisher, which is wild-caught salmon rolled in phyllo and baked in the shape of a fish with lightly sautéed vegetables and dill aioli. Plates are adorned with blooms from the floral shop.

Clockwise, from top left: This lovely tea room is attached to a florist and gift shop. Rather than tiny tea sandwiches, the menu here includes comforting entrées like the Chateau Earl Gray. The Kingfisher is a signature item of wild-caught salmon rolled in phyllo dough. Several little nooks can be found throughout the dining area to leisurely sip a cup of tea.

Other entrées include a house-made ricotta gnocchi, vegetable-filled crepes, and a chicken breast with honey dijon sauce. A light house salad, a chicken salad, and a chicken pot pie soup round out the menu. You can also add a scone with clotted cream and jam to your meal.

For the little ones, there are also children's meal selections of macaroni and cheese or chicken nuggets.

Shop for gourmet teas and other gift items in the floral/gift shop or online through their website.

The tearoom is open for lunch service only from Wednesday through Saturday.

7005 Madison St., Merrillville, 219-769-3454
merrillvillefloristandtearoom.com

JUNK DITCH BREWING COMPANY

The most impressive meal you'll ever have at a craft brewery

A trio who was running a food truck and baked goods company came together to launch Junk Ditch Brewing Company, an oasis of craft beer and creative, scratch-made food in a cool historic building. Andrew Smith, Dan Campbell, and Grace Kelly May brought their passion for hospitality and an everything-from-scratch philosophy in creating this space of good food, good beer, and good vibes.

Located in the century-old former Korte Paper Company warehouse, the place has that cool industrial feel with exposed brick and Edison lighting. The brewery's name comes from a tributary of the St. Marys River than runs behind the building.

About a dozen beers can be found on tap, from IPAs to lagers to porters and stouts available in a flight pour or full pour. They also carry guest brews, and for those who aren't beer drinkers, you can enjoy a glass of wine from France, Italy, or Spain.

Like a lot of craft breweries it has an eclectic mix of menu items. You'll find a diverse bunch of cultural influences in perusing the menu, from a Cuban sandwich to banh mi to a Greek pita on the lunch menu.

One thing you won't want to miss is the wood-fired pizza. It's not your standard cheese and pepperoni. Well, they do serve a cheese and pepperoni, but that's not all it is. Along with pepperoni are pickled

Check out their second location, the Junk Ditch Huntington Tap.

Left: The interior of this century-old building includes exposed brick, creating an attractive backdrop in the dining area. *Top right:* A fisherman stew is a satisfying, hearty meal made by their creative chef. *Bottom right:* Be sure to try a flight of their several varieties of craft beer available on tap daily.

jalapeños and chili honey. A sausage and mushroom pizza is made with mozzarella, gourmet mushrooms, onion soubise, truffle Yuma vinaigrette, and arugula. They're bursting with flavors you didn't know existed.

Soups and salads are way beyond the norm in such a good way. Carrot rillettes, microgreens, lemon agrodolce, truffle vinaigrette, and dill oil are a few of the ingredients you'll find. And they make the most of seasonal abundance. For a very brief time in the spring, you can enjoy morels with polenta, ragout, mushroom aioli, wild onion cream, and microgreens. It's food you'd expect to find in exclusive, top-tier, award-winning fine-dining establishments rather than in a craft brewery.

Also, keep them in mind for weekend brunch when you'll find many of your favorites with a twist or you can be introduced to some great new ethnic dishes.

1825 W Main St., Fort Wayne, 260-203-4045
junkditchbrewingco.com

OASIS DINER

The perfect blast from the past

If you drive down Main Street in Plainfield, you'll be lured in by the glow of neon to an oasis—one that takes you back to simpler times and wraps you in a big, nostalgic hug. Oasis Diner is that oasis. With throwback decor in this genuine retro diner, a menu of classics, and music that makes you want to shake a tail feather, it's a place to go where you simply can't be sad. The surroundings don't allow it.

Oasis Diner, manufactured by Mountain View Diners in Signac, New Jersey, was shipped via railroad to the east side of Plainfield in 1954. Original owners were James Canavan and Frank Thurber. Thurber operated it until selling it in the 1970s. It went through a few other owners before closing in 2008.

In 2010, Indiana Landmarks listed the diner on their "10 Most Endangered Indiana Buildings" list. This listing prompted the Town of Plainfield to conduct a feasibility study on the possible relocation of the diner to their recently revitalized town center.

Local residents Doug Huff and Don Rector stepped in with plans to restore and reopen this historical landmark. After more than three years of research, planning, and construction, Oasis Diner reopened in 2014.

Both the exterior and interior of Oasis Diner have been restored back to their original appearance. It's so spot-on that you almost feel guilty parking a modern car in the lot beside this beauty rather than a sleek, oversized mid-century Chevy with dramatic fins and artistic headlights. The diner remains located on the Historic National Road and is the

> Be sure to try a mug of their handcrafted root beer, which is available in 64-ounce to-go growlers. And for a supersweet treat, try the butterscotch root beer.

Left: The walls are lined with bits of nostalgia, including historic photos of the diner. *Center:* The exterior and interior of the Oasis Diner were restored to their original appearance before re-opening in 2014, which included neon signs. *Right:* One of their most popular items is the Hoosier favorite, the breaded pork tenderloin.

only diner on the National Road in Indiana. It is one of less than five historical diners to remain on US 40 from Cumberland, Maryland, to Vandalia, Illinois.

This place is vintage through and through with throwback counter seats, a lunch box collection covering the walls, and a variety of vintage ads hanging in the bathroom.

Now, let's get to the food! Oasis Diner is a place where you can get breakfast, lunch, or dinner. The breakfast menu has all the mandatory standards of a good breakfast place, like pancakes, omelets, and hash. There are a half dozen "National Road Specials," like the Atlantic City Stuffed French Toast, the Kansas City Loaded Biscuits and Gravy, and the San Francisco Avocado Toast. The signature breakfast entrée, however, is the Indianapolis Country Fried Breakfast. It consists of a fried tenderloin (or chicken breast) covered with sausage gravy and served with two eggs, home fries, and toast.

Lunch and dinner service starts at 11 a.m. with plenty of deep-fried favorites to start with. The tenderloin is the centerpiece of the menu, and it's served just like you'd expect one to be in the Hoosier state— fried to golden perfection with a hearty crunch hanging way over the sides of a brioche bun.

Other enticing sandwiches include the Oasis Burger with their house-made pulled pork, bacon, barbecue sauce coleslaw, pickles, and cheddar cheese served on a brioche bun; a Philly cheesesteak; deluxe grilled cheese; and Reuben.

405 W Main St., Plainfield, 317-837-7777
oasisdiner.com

ABBOTT'S CANDIES

Indiana's oldest candy shop

There's no doubt that a box of handmade, gooey, nutty, sugary chocolates makes your life sweeter. There's no better way to give your life that lift than at Abbott's Candies.

The business was started in 1890 by Willam Clay Abbott, known as W. C. Abbott, who had been a top traveling salesman for a local candy manufacturer, Dilling Candy Company. He held onto a dream of one day making his own candy brand. He first went the direction of opening a restaurant, specializing in fried chicken, steak, short orders, and pastries. Word of mouth led to a request for him to serve the Indiana State Fair Board and honored guests.

Around this time, he began experimenting with candy and ice cream making, and his first creation was Abbott's butterscotch. Next came the chocolate drop. With demand for candy ramping up, he abandoned the restaurant business to focus solely on candy making. His second manufacturing location was a converted garage in his backyard, which remained in use until 1985.

The business remained in the family through three generations, and with the untimely deaths of W. C. and then his son, Bruce, their two widows dedicated themselves to keeping the tradition going. They added a retail space and gift shop, and the business opened additional locations through a licensing agreement.

As the business moved into a third century of candy making, a new family purchased the company in 2012 and continues to operate it

> **Among the items on display in the store is a thank-you note to the owners written by Bob Hope.**

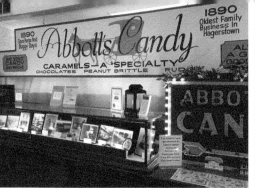

Left: The exterior of the current candy shop which was once a church. *Center:* At the candy counter, you can buy treats that taste the same as if you would have bought them back in 1890. *Right:* Some of the original and long-used equipment can be viewed when visiting Abbott's Candies.

today. Jay and Lynn Noel and their sons, Jason and Ryan, are now two generations of a second family operating the 130-plus-year-old company.

In 1985, after a fire destroyed their retail store, they purchased a 19th-century building that had served as a former church and then garage, car wash, car dealership, and machine warehouse. It became the new store and factory, and it is where the company remains.

Candies are still produced the old-fashioned way, with an original candy cutter that is still in use today and other equipment that has been used for decades. Caramels are a treat you just have to try. They're made the same way they have been made since Abbott's early days. And it isn't just plain caramels you'll find here. They also make sea salt, nut, and cream puff caramels.

There are too many treats to mention, but you can be assured that every truffle, piece of toffee, chunk of brittle, or chocolate-covered cream is made carefully and with pride and love.

While you can easily order their treats online and have them delivered, a visit to their brick-and-mortar location is a fun trip down memory lane. It feels like a museum and a step back in time. You may be lucky enough to be there when candy production is happening. There are also some fun historical displays for viewing.

48 E Walnut St., Hagerstown, 877-801-1200
abbottscandy.com

RUSTED SILO

Award-winning, finger-licking, small-town barbecue

After traveling and cooking all over the world, Robert Ecker looked forward to settling down in a place where he could bring his love of food to others. Back in 1992, he even made his way to France to help open the culinary part of Euro Disney. He also spent time in the Panama Beach brewery scene before taking the leap to open his own place with his wife, Tina, in Lizton.

In opening the space, the couple decided to do one thing and do it well: barbecue. And boy do they do it well. They do it so well that it's been voted "Best BBQ in Indianapolis" several times by readers of the *Indy Star*.

All of the side dishes and desserts are made from scratch using family recipes. Brisket and pork are slow smoked for 12 hours. Quality ingredients and simple but thorough cooking methods make this such a standout place.

Ecker's mother-in-law is the pie maker, creating scrumptious bourbon pecan pie, peach cobbler, and sugar cream pie as well as Mama June's Nanner Puddin' (banana pudding).

As you dine, you can watch meats slowly rotate on a carousel behind the counter, and all the care that goes into its preparation is evident when you take that first bite. From pulled pork to house-made chorizo to brisket to chicken, each is an explosion of flavor in your mouth, especially when you slather it in one of their own sauces.

No shortcuts are taken on their wonderfully Southern sides, either. Potato salad is made with tender-boiled Idaho potatoes mixed with Duke's mayonnaise and French's mustard, diced veggies, relish, and a little cane sugar. Collard greens are chopped and cooked with ham

Left: A variety of housemade sauces are available to accompany your meats. *Center:* A platter of meats and sides are sure to satisfy. *Right:* Owners Robert and Tina Ecker show off one of the pecan pies they serve at the restaurant.

hocks, bacon, and onions. Cheese grits are made with Kentucky-grown and -milled non-GMO corn; simmered with butter, cream, and milk; and finished with freshly grated sharp cheddar. The Mac-n-Beer cheese is super creamy, made with three cheeses and a splash of beer, and my favorite feature is the handful of Goldfish crackers on top.

The "Ranch Beans" are a bit different than baked beans, inspired by the pot of beans that would be kept warm on the fire at all times during cattle drives in the West, with ingredients being added to provide cow hands with a hearty meal. This version combines pinto beans with chunky bits of tomato, pepper, onions, jalapeños, bacon, and smoked brisket. The rusty exterior and design of the building almost make it seem like it could be situated in a tiny outpost out west.

They've got a nice selection of craft beers as well, because is there a better combination than beer and barbecue?

A railroad runs alongside the building, so close that you feel the rumbling as it goes by. Sometimes it parks next to the building so the train crew can grab a bite, and sometimes they even preorder and the meal is run out to their window—the coolest drive-through ever.

411 N State St., Lizton, 317-994-6145
rustedsilobrewhouse.com

THE TIN PLATE FINE FOOD AND SPIRITS

Best tenderloin in Madison County

If there's one thing Hoosiers take seriously, it's their breaded pork tenderloin. The Tin Plate tenderloin is one of the best you will find anywhere. It's topped the "Best of Madison County" list in the *Herald Bulletin* and has been a longtime customer favorite.

The sandwich is a 10-ounce tenderloin pounded so thin that it easily doubles the size of the bun it sits on. It is set apart by a secret breading blend that gives it an ultra crunch. Each year the restaurant serves about six tons of pork tenderloin, which translates to about 20,000 individual servings. Owner Patrick Rice went to great pains to perfect the recipe, and he landed on pure pork perfection.

The Tin Plate has a connection to the fascinating history of the American Tin Plate company in Elwood, which dates back to the early 1890s. It was the first complete tin mill constructed after the McKinley Tariff Act of 1899 and the first place in the US to do tinning. Previously, most tin products were imported from Wales. The mill operated until 1938.

The restaurant and bar are in a building that sat across from the mill property and was built in the 1920s. Bits of the company's history are spread throughout the eatery.

Today it's a place where you can bring the family in for a meal that won't break the bank, you can bring a group for an event in the private room, or you can sit at the bar with a brew and a hearty plate.

Left: A plate of barbecue pulled pork nachos is displayed in front of a restaurant sign. *Top right:* The Tin Plate is known for their oversized breaded pork tenderloin prepared with their special coating recipe. *Bottom right:* The dining room includes pieces of memorabilia from the American Tin Plate Company in Elwood, including this vintage sign.

While the tenderloin is their biggest standout menu item, there's much more to choose from. Fried appetizers filled with pickles and onions and jalapeños make up the appetizer menu along with their popular ribbon fries.

Another signature item that should be on your radar is the roast beef Manhattan. Instead of a traditional beef gravy, Rice created a unique tomato gravy using tomatoes from Red Gold, who has a production site just down the road in Elwood. Now that's local!

2233 S J St., Elwood, 765-557-8231

In honor of all those who served in the military who are still MIA (missing in action) or POW (prisoners of war), a Missing Man Table sits in the corner of the restaurant throughout the year.

PERILLO'S PIZZERIA

Native of Italy serving up Italian specialties in small town

Don't you love when you find a hidden food gem in an unexpected place? In the small town of North Salem with a population of under 500, Damiano Perillo and his family serve up specialties that he learned to make in his hometown in Sicily. He attended culinary school in Palermo and came to the United States in 1999. In 2011, he opened the restaurant. His wife is from the area, and that's what led him to make the move to Indiana.

In the pizzeria, only fresh, high-quality ingredients are used, and much of it is sourced from the family's own garden. What Perillo doesn't grow, he tries to purchase locally when possible. Only the best goes into the New York, Sicilian, and stuffed pizza that is created in artisan style, fresh to order.

Each day, every ingredient is chopped and sliced. Sauce is made fresh each morning. You can expect a meal that is scratch-made and food that is fresh out of the oven.

The building that Perillo's is housed in dates back to the 1890s. It was the medical office of Dr. Oscar H. Wiseheart for more than 60 years and later was used as a feed store and a saloon before being converted into an apartment. Perillo's family did all the renovation work to the building themselves before opening. Part of those renovations included laying brick for an outdoor patio that is a popular spot for alfresco dining in warmer months.

Leave the plastic at home. Perillo's is a cash-only establishment. A 24-hour ATM is located just a block away.

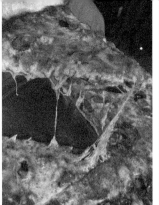

Left: Cannoli is one of the dessert selections at Perillo's Pizzeria. *Center:* A cheesy slice of pie reminiscent of what Damiano Perillo learned to make in Sicily. *Right:* A serving of garlic knots with a cup of homemade marinara for dipping are a perfect way to start a visit.

Be sure to come hungry when you visit because there's a menu of carb-filled delights calling your name. Start out with the garlic rolls with marinara that melt in your mouth. If you're a fan of mussels, you'll definitely want to give Perillo's a try; they're served with garlic bread that you'll want to use to soak up every last bit of that sauce. The portobello al forno is a full-of-flavor vegetarian item baked with fresh spinach and mozzarella cheese.

Do not sleep on those homemade meatballs that are such a fine consistency and served in a pool of their housemade marinara. Get them on their own or pair them with a plate of pasta. (You can do half orders of pasta dishes!) They also offer gluten-free pasta options, so everyone can enjoy it.

The New York–style pizza comes in only one size with eight large slices, and they offer a few specialty pizzas, like the melanzane pizza of with ricotta, eggplant, basil, and mozzarella; the margherita pizza; or the chicken alfredo pizza with chicken, spinach, bacon, and sun-dried tomatoes. New York style is also available by the slice. A meat-stuffed double-crust pizza, a Sicilian deep dish, and a gluten-free cauliflower parmesan crust are additonal pizza choices. They even have a keto pizza with a crust made from chia seeds, almond flour, cream cheese, and mozzarella.

5 S Broadway St., North Salem, 765-676-4171

BLUE GATE RESTAURANT

Amish-style restaurant serves up comfort food

Known for its Amish-style cooking, Blue Gate Restaurant & Bakery is a destination restaurant. It draws people from far and wide to sit down for a meal. Some are also there for a show in the Blue Gate Music Hall, some are there as part of a day trip or weekend getaway to experience Amish country, some make it an eating/shopping excursion, and then there are those who are there simply for the food.

The award-winning restaurant offers a cozy atmosphere where you can enjoy homestyle Amish food with friendly service. It's part of the Riegsecker Marketplace, which got its beginning in 1984.

Mel Riegsecker's father was an Amish harness maker who taught his son everything he knew. In 1970, Mel made a miniature wagon and horses with hitches in great detail. After his father displayed it in his shop, he soon got an offer to purchase it. Realizing there was a market for the scaled-down wagon model hobby of his, he continued making them and selling them. A buyer from the Sears catalog discovered his work, and it was soon his full-time business.

When he discovered that people also liked watching him work in his shop, he knew it was time to move somewhere larger. In 1984, Mel and his wife, June, purchased and renovated an old factory building in Shipshewana and called it the Craft Barn. It soon grew to have additional shops, a restaurant, a bakery, a theater, a carriage business, and a hotel.

The restaurant opened near the Craft Barn as a small 50-seat dining room. It expanded to 105 seats and two dining rooms later on, but after 20 years, they knew they'd outgrown the space. The old building was torn down and replaced as a new 750-seat eatery with six dining rooms, a bakery, and a theater.

Left: Over two dozen pie offerings can be found at Blue Gate Restaurant, including the popular Red Raspberry Cream. *Center:* Stop in the bakery for fresh pies, breads, cookies and more. *Right:* Have Thanksgiving dinner at any time when you visit the Blue Gate and order the roast turkey dinner.

Using local recipes of Amish/Mennonite dishes, Blue Gate is the place to go in Shipshewana for a dose of comfort food. There are three ways to dine there. You can order off the menu, opt for Blue Gate's Famous Family Style, or have an all-you-can-eat Amish buffet.

Among the favorite dinner entrées are fried chicken, country roast beef, homestyle meat loaf, slow-roasted smoked ham, chicken and biscuits, and roasted turkey dinner.

The buffet has varied items, but you'll always find fried chicken and roast beef along with a large number of sides made from scratch and a dessert bar. On Saturdays, they offer a breakfast buffet, as well.

About 25 pies are offered at any given time, including some fresh seasonal flavors, with the top five sellers being cherry, Dutch apple, red raspberry cream, chocolate, and peanut butter. Stop in the bakery to take home a pie, cookies, bread, jams, peanut butter, apple butter, and more.

195 N Van Buren St., Shipshewana, 260-768-4725
thebluegate.com

Shop while you wait. You'll find a sizable gift shop off the lobby, and there's an intercom system throughout the shop so you'll be able to hear your name being called when your table is ready.

CINDY'S DINER

Serving the world, 15 at a time

Cindy's Diner is small but mighty. The little 15-seat diner was purchased in 1952 by Noah Clauss, and it became one of Fort Wayne's first fast food restaurants. It's changed hands a few times over the years, for a time being known as Paul's Diner and then Marge's Diner before a 1990 restoration and renaming to Cindy's Diner. It's also been moved twice: in 1966 and then again in 2014 to its current location at the corner of Maiden Lane and Berry Street. Longtime employee Angie Rowedda bought the business in 2016 after 20 years of serving up hungry diners in the small space.

The quarters are so tight that private conversations aren't really a thing. You'll find regulars talking across the counter from one end to the other about their families, the news, or what model of truck they drive. It harkens back to a time long ago when everyone knew everyone, and if you walked in as strangers, you left as friends. When the weather is warm and you want to spread out a little, there are a handful of tables for outdoor dining.

The set-up also allows for you to watch your food cooked on a griddle right in front of you. You get your food piping hot as it only has to be passed a few feet to the counter.

You can order breakfast any time they are open from their nine selections of breakfast specialties, including corned beef hash, country sausage gravy and biscuits, french toast, or different variations of eggs with toast, potatoes, or meat. The most popular by far is the Garbage, a blend of eggs, potatoes, cheese, onions, and bits of ham. À la carte breakfast items of hotcakes, breads, meats, and more can be selected to build a meal.

Top left: Homemade biscuits and gravy are among the breakfast options. *Bottom left:* Pies are made from scratch with the pecan pie being a big seller. *Right:* The small 15-seat diner has been moved a couple times before landing at its current location.

A long list of sandwiches await you, from a grilled chicken breast to a fish sandwich to a club or BLT. Most popular are the burgers and the pork tenderloin, which you can get grilled or breaded. A local butcher sources the pork, which is hand pounded and breaded. Homemade soups are a great way to warm up on a cold day.

Pie is homemade with about 20 different varieties being made from recipes of the former owners. Peanut butter is the all-time favorite, but customers also enjoy the butterscotch, rhubarb, and chocolate cream.

There's not a parking lot, but it's usually not too hard to find street parking. Just be aware that there are meters on area streets that you'll have to feed.

230 W Berry St., Fort Wayne, 260-422-1957

Don't pass up the creamy shakes that are hand dipped and made the old-fashioned way in their vintage stainless steel multimixer.

RH INDIANAPOLIS

Former DeHaan Estate now a gallery for RH luxury brand with dining room

You'll be transported to a world of elegance as soon as you pull off the road and into the gates where you'll follow a long road to this mansion turned swanky restaurant-showroom.

RH was formerly known as Restoration Hardware, the world's leading luxury home furnishings purveyor, offering furniture, lighting, textiles, bath ware, decor, outdoor furnishings, and more. The company was founded in California in 1979. In 2015, it opened its first hospitality concept in Chicago and since then has added more than a dozen restaurants inside select RH galleries.

In 2022, the Linden House in Indianapolis was sold and leased to RH. It was the home of the late Christel DeHaan, a businesswoman and philanthropist, constructed in 2007. The 42,000-square-foot mansion sits on a 151-acre site that once served as the site of a Benedictine monastery and is surrounded by gardens and sculptures with a 35-acre private lake.

The 60-room property, one of the most accurate Palladian-style villas to exist in the United States, is now a design and hospitality destination integrating RH collections with rare art and antiques. Front and center as you enter the estate is the dining room and the Lakeside Terrace and Wine Bar that looks out onto the lake and stunning landscape.

The dining room is an immersive space that feels more like a museum than a room to sit and have lunch in. It has soaring windows and boasts a lighting installation by master glass designer Alison Berger. There are marble tables, gold-rimmed mirrors, Edison lighting, simple muted furniture, and sculptures in each corner.

Left: RH Indianapolis serves as a showroom for RH products and houses a dining room in this former mansion. *Top right:* The Gem Salad with Green Goddess dressing is a popular menu item. *Bottom right:* A bedroom showroom in the mansion.

The menu has a carefully curated collection of elegant classics and an impressive list of champagnes and fine wines from around the world. While the menu is brief, it hits all the points of an establishment of its caliber, serving dips with caviar as an introduction, artisanal charcuterie and cheese boards, fresh creative salads, elevated sandwiches, prime steak cuts, truffled fries, and decadent desserts.

A meal at RH Indianapolis is absolutely something any foodie, historian, or architecture buff needs to experience at least once.

Allow time to peruse the many staged rooms of RH furnishings and accessories and take a walk on the grounds.

4501 N Michigan Rd., Indianapolis, 317-706-9670
rh.com/us/en/indianapolis

LITTLE ITALY

Chef-owned eatery offers authentic family-style Italian cuisine

When Andrew and Theresa Easterday moved from Chicago to the suburbs, they missed having little independently run neighborhood trattorias nearby to enjoy a fresh, casual, quality meal. So, they decided to open one.

A graduate of the Cooking & Hospitality Institute of Chicago, Andrew Easterday began his career working as a chef in a boutique Italian restaurant in Chicago. To expand his culinary repertoire, the restaurant's manager sent him to Italy several times, where he honed his skills in kitchens.

Since 2014, he's brought that experience and passion to Little Italy, where everything is made from scratch. The only thing you'll find in the freezer is ice cream.

Set back in a little strip mall along the busy Route 30, it doesn't immediately catch your eye from the outside when driving by. But once you're inside, you realize that magic is happening here.

Homemade pastas are prepared daily and are a big part of the menu, available in "Little Italy" or "Big Italy" portion sizes. From rigatoni to alfredo to ziti to penne, each is blended with different vegetables and creamy, made-from-scratch sauces. There's also a scrumptious lasagna layered with a rich veal bolognese and three cheeses, and a special handmade ravioli is featured each week. Entrées also come with a platter of baked ziti.

You'll find traditional Italian favorites at their best, items like chicken or eggplant parmesan and sausage and peppers. A crispy tomato-braised pork shoulder is their bestseller. Choice steaks and hand-cut and deboned fish fillets will wow you.

Left: Casual, but classy and clean, Little Italy gives friendly vibes that make you feel like you're at home. *Top right:* A shot of samples from the menu. Credit to Little Italy. *Bottom right:* Don't forget a glass of wine to accompany your meal.

It's also a great place to enjoy a thin and crispy Neapolitan-style pizza on freshly made hand-tossed dough and cooked in a brick oven. There's a half dozen specialty options or you can build your own. They also have a gluten-free version.

The Easterdays pride themselves on being affordable. By being a scratch kitchen and not purchasing prepared foods, they are able to keep costs down and pass savings on to the customer.

1155 Joliet St., Dyer, 219-865-3040
dyerlittleitaly.com

Join the text club to get daily specials delivered to your inbox.

VERA MAE'S BISTRO

Upscale cuisine in Muncie's downtown historic district

Vera Mae's opened in 1999, but it's housed in a building that had already been there for a century. When a former bakery storefront was purchased and renovated by founder Kent Shuff, it was the start of the revitalization of Muncie's historic district.

A plaque hangs on the front of the structure noting the designation of an Althea Stoeckel Award for preservation efforts. The restaurant expanded later to add the former Ballard Hardware space next door, naming the dining room Ballaird Hall.

The building has a charming vintage facade, original tin ceilings, and some paneling and light fixtures that were rescued from the original courthouse in Muncie. A vintage-looking bar was actually custom made by a local expert woodworker and is a beautiful backdrop for the Ballaird Hall dining room. The basement houses a wine cellar and a private dining room.

The restaurant was named for Shuff's grandmother with some dishes inspired by her cooking but perfected by the current chef. The varied menu covers dishes of various ethnicities. Popular entrées include a dill-crusted cod and chicken marcona. Additional specialties include jagerschnitzel, hollandaise chicken, and truffle linguini de parma.

Steak and seafood options are impressive. In addition to the regular menu items, they offer a weekly fresh fish feature. The seared scallop appetizer wrapped in bacon and served over grilled kale with lemon butter and Peppadew peppers is a must-try. Scallops can also be added to your steak, or you can opt for Oscar-style with lump crab and hollandaise.

Top left: A nostalgic storefront graces the front of the building. *Top right:* Dim, soft lighting creates an intimate ambiance. *Bottom left:* A number of luxurious entrées, like the Filet Oscar, can be savored with a glass of wine. *Bottom center:* Among the starters menu is bacon-wrapped scallops. *Bottom right:* French onion soup is served with scissors to cut the thick strings of melted cheese.

A couple signature items should not be missed: Vera's french onion soup, which comes with a pair of scissors for cutting the thick, gooey Gruyère, and Vera's classic bread pudding made with bananas and cranberries, served warm and topped with a whiskey sauce.

A recent addition is a kids' menu, making the place more welcoming for families with some nice child-friendly options.

If you're looking for lodging while in town, you may want to consider renting out the expansive second floor above the restaurant, the Residence at Vera Mae's, which can sleep six.

209 S Walnut St., Muncie, 765-767-5544
veramaes.com

TEIBEL'S FAMILY RESTAURANT

Fourth-generation family restaurant known for lake perch

Going strong after 95 years in business, Teibel's is one of the Calumet region's oldest eateries. It opened its doors at the corner of Routes 30 and 41 in 1929 as a simple 12-seat highway diner. Now it's a large full-service family restaurant with multiple rooms and banquet halls that can seat up to 400. The café room is more on the casual side, while the formal dining room offers a cozy and upscale atmosphere with the feel of a supper club.

Brothers Martin and Stephen Teibel started out selling sandwiches and homemade fried chicken, but the menu has evolved to include recipes influenced by their Austrian heritage. They still serve up a mean sandwich, like the club, the Italian beef, the Reuben, and more unique ones like tomato basil grilled cheese and the walleye po'boy.

Chicken is still a popular entrée, but you can also find additional comfort foods, like roast turkey and homemade chicken pot pie, and harder-to-find nostalgic plates like chicken liver and onions. Broiled steaks range from a petite filet to chop steak to a Kansas City strip.

Since those modest early days, they've also become known as a top destination for seafood in the area, serving their extremely popular Canadian lake perch along with Lake Erie walleye filets and Indonesian frog legs.

> Try and plan your visit during the holiday season when the entire restaurant, inside and out, is decked out in high fashion.

Left: An institution in Northwest Indiana, Teibel's has been feeding hungry diners since opening in 1929. Credit Teibel's Restaurant. *Right:* Teibel's has long been known for their fried perch. Credit Teibel's Restaurant.

Catering has become a big business, and their stuffed mushroom caps are an appetizer that is highly requested. Other starters run the gamut from crab cakes to shrimp cocktail to onion rings to fried green tomatoes. But you may not have room for them following the old-school relish tray of coleslaw, pickled beets, and cottage cheese.

The rolls are so good, they've made their way onto local store shelves to be heated at home. Entrées and classic dinners include a scoop of ice cream for dessert. You'll find a nice selection of local craft beers on tap, a sizable spirits list, and a craft cocktail list with several classics and others with a twist.

As it heads toward a century in business, Teibel's has remained a family business through four generations, and Stephen Teibel's great-grandson is now at the helm.

1775 US-41, Schererville, 219-865-2000

FIREHOUSE BBQ & BLUES

A barbecue haven where food and music mesh

It's always fun to find good food in a really cool place. And when that really cool place is an 1860s firehouse, you know the barbecue will be smokin'. Located in Richmond's Historic Depot District, the building sat vacant for about a decade before undergoing a two-year restoration and being converted into a restaurant. Part of the renovation included an extremely realistic exterior mural that makes it appear as if smoke and fire are coming out of the windows.

Originally firefighters Tom Boles and Rick Bolen were the ones to see the potential and renovate the building. It has since changed to new ownership of Nick Arborgast and Dustin Gavin. The duo continue to make it a place for people to get together over good food and take in some good live music. They call their passion project a "true celebration of flavor, music, and community."

The limestone exterior and interior hardwood floors with exposed brick create a cool vibe. The signature fire pole in the dining room is an added bonus. The dining room portion of the building was once the bay from which horses pulled the engine from to fight fires. The building continued to operate as a firehouse until 1930. From there it was a community center and meeting space for the local American Legion post.

The entertainment schedule is full of local talent of varying genres, and karaoke takes place weekly for those who want to show off their pipes. Richmond has a rich musical history, and throughout the space you'll see quotes from well-known musical artists.

Aside from the historic surroundings and talent that you'll find onstage, Firehouse serves some darned good barbecue. It's done the way barbecue should be—low and slow to seal in all that flavor and produce a juicy and tender end result.

Left: Much of the original woodwork is visible inside. *Center:* A historic 1860s firehouse is the setting for this barbecue and blues joint. *Right:* A mural on the side of the restaurant depicts a building on fire.

Pulled pork, barbecue ribs, and brisket are some of the most popular of the meat offerings. Each one is smoked over hickory for 14 hours, and brisket is hand trimmed. A big chicken dinner of whole smoked breast and the Porkzilla, a large smoke chop, will fill the largest of appetites.

You'll also want to try their Mexican-inspired specialties: the Smokehouse tacos with choice of meat, the Tex Mex Wrap with chicken or pork, and Pamela's PortBliss fajitas.

The appetizers are called "first alarms," and the one that really carries out the barbecue theme is the huge plate of pulled pork barbecue nachos. Firehouse pizzas are made to order with sauces and smoky meats. The jacket potatoes are a meal on their own. Called Texas Taters, the meats and chili spill way over with veggies and tangy sauce.

You can't have good barbecue without good sides. Mac and cheese, scalloped cabbage, sweet potato casserole, and baked beans are a few of the scrumptious sides to accompany your entrées.

400 N 8th St., Richmond, 765-598-5440
thefirehousebbqandblues.com

You can also get your barbecue fix at their new Dunkirk location.

GOSHEN BREWING CO.

Family-friendly brewery's menu highlights local foods

Have you ever been to a brewery where there was parking outside specifically for horses? That's just one of the things that makes this brewery a little different. The surrounding rural area is dotted with Amish farms, and it's not unusual to make your way to Goshen Brewing to have a pint and see a beautiful horse attached to a black buggy outside.

The brick structure is an old power company building adjacent to a pump house on the Elkhart River. Owners Jesse and Amanda Sensenig moved to Colorado for grad school in 2005 and fell in love with the beer scene where there were the most breweries per capita at the time. They later moved to Ohio, where Jesse did home brewing and got experience working with a local brewer. When there was an opportunity to purchase the NIPSCo building that had sat vacant since the 1990s, they were all in.

In the taproom you can look down through windows at the brewing floor or get a peek in the kitchen at the food elevator that transports meals down from the second-floor kitchen. The brewery opened in 2015, and in 2018 a beer hall was added with garage doors that open to a patio area. In cooler weather, you can hang out in a heated igloo.

The beer hall is a happening place with weekly live entertainment and a monthly vinyl night where different people come to spin tunes. It's a family-friendly spot where you can grab board games to play at the tables.

The menu has a creative mix of dishes, some that are Asian inspired. But each one has a little bit of a twist from what you'd typically expect. The majority of the menu items are made from scratch in-house using as many local, organic ingredients as they can get.

Left: Additional seating can be found in the outdoor patio space. *Center:* The historic building has an add on with lots of light and garage doors that open seasonally during good weather. *Right:* A variety of craft beers are brewed at Goshen Brewing. Try a flight of six of their on-tap brews.

For starters you can choose from shishito poppers that are charred with onions and bacon and served over a tangy goat cheese sauce or tofu ssam, which is a blackened tofu with caramelized onions, pickled radishes, marinated bean sprouts, mustard seed sauce, soy ginger sauce, and Bibb lettuce. If you're more traditional, pick the french fries, chips, or mac and cheese, which is best with barbecued pulled pork or brisket.

Popular sandwiches are the Carolina Gold smoked pork shoulder with coleslaw and Carolina gold mustard on brioche; a grilled cheese sandwich stuffed with goat cheese, rosemary, fig jam, and Amish cheese; and the Thai'd chicken, topped with Thai chili jam, sweet cabbage slaw, sriracha, and aioli on a brioche bun.

The Thai rice bowl is filled with pickled shallots, boiled egg, cucumbers, oyster mushrooms, and more with limited availability. And while other places may have a taco Tuesday, Goshen's has pad thai Tuesday.

A dozen of their beers are on tap, ranging from pale ales to lagers to stouts and everything in between. Bring a friend, and if you each order a six-glass flight, you can make your way through them all.

315 W Washington St., Goshen, 574-971-5324
goshenbrewing.com

THE PREWITT RESTAURANT AND LOUNGE

Former movie theater sees new life as restaurant, lounge, entertainment venue

There was a time when the future of this historic 1927 theater was unknown. It sat vacant for about six years before being converted into a restaurant with a small stage and a cocktail lounge. The movie theme is carried through at this upscale eatery of American fare where the stage/screen is used for live entertainment and showing classic black-and-white films. It's located in the heart of historic downtown Plainfield, just west of Indianapolis.

In the main dining room, you'll find a sunken area with tables and a lounge area with plush leather couches. There's an upstairs dining area with a private bar that gives the vibes of a vintage speakeasy.

The dinner menu is separated into clever sections with previews (appetizers), main features (entrées), and credits (desserts). There's a creative array of dishes, from beef short ribs with crispy polenta and butterscotch barbecue to duck porchetta with roasted squash puree, pomegranate sherry gastrique, and pistachio gremolata. The descriptions sound elaborate, and the flavors are mind-blowing.

Lunch menu offerings include a variety of sandwiches and salads. Try the Godfather (full of Italian meats, provolone, tomato, onion, shrettuce, pepper relish, and basil aioli on an Italian roll) or chicken ballerini (an herbs de Provence-marinated local chicken breast, spicy fire-roasted tomato sugo, Italian cheeses, and basil caper pistou on grilled bread).

Brunch includes some really amazing menu items that go way beyond what you could imagine—things like shrimp avocado toast

Left to right: If you're looking for something sharable, try one of their charcuterie platters served on a lazy Susan board. The former theater is a nice setting for a weekend brunch. The former movie theater marquee now features the name of the Prewitt Restaurant and Lounge. Beer flights are served in old movie reels.

with poblano ceviche, avocado mousse, grapefruit, and lemon aioli on sourdough.

Green Eggs and Ham are made with a smoked porterhouse chop, butter-beer-glazed wilted pepper cress with crispy potatoes, and two sunny-side eggs. The Prewitt Burger has two locally-raised, dry-aged beef patties on a brioche bun with white cheddar cheese, jalapeño bacon jam, caramelized onion, shrettuce, and black garlic aioli with tallow fries on the side. Hungry yet?

A great way to start is with Meat + Cheese, a lovely charcuterie platter with cheeses, pickled vegetables, crackers, jam, and nuts and a beer flight that is served in an old movie reel with some snack mix.

You'll find the most unique presentations in things like Lox Waffles with Balmoral smoked salmon, Calabrian chili cream cheese, pickled onion, crispy capers, and cured egg yolk or the Bee + Gee buttermilk biscuits smothered in sausage gravy topped with pickled onions and microgreens. The chef's creativity was working overtime in preparing this menu.

On the stage and patio are an eclectic lineup of performers. They also host trivia nights and other events throughout the year.

121 W Main St., 1st fl., Plainfield, 317-203-5240
prewittdining.com

MUG-N-BUN

Nostalgic drive-in still has meals delivered via carhops

In 1960, the iconic Mug-n-Bun debuted in the shadow of the Indianapolis Motor Speedway. The town of Speedway is a place where there's an intense love of cars, and where better to blend cars and food than at a fun drive-in with inexpensive food brought out to your vehicle by a carhop? It initially opened in 1956 and was operated for the first four years as Frostop.

Some things have changed over the years and some things haven't. You can still have your order taken and meal brought out to you without getting out of your car by turning on headlights to summon a carhop. You can also dine on the patio if you prefer. After years of closing down in winter months, an adjacent building was converted into a dining room that allows the business to go year-round. Plenty of vintage decor inside adds to the nostalgic vibes. A vintage neon sign outside has an arrow directing you into the parking lot.

The menu boasts that Mug-n-Bun is the "oldest and finest drive-in restaurant in Indianapolis." As you'd expect, they serve up a variety of classic diner food and Midwestern staples. Burgers and fries. A breaded pork tenderloin. Hand-cut and dipped onion rings. Coney dogs. Chili cheese fries. Grilled cheese. Fried fish. Polish sausage. Classic frosty milkshakes and more.

Mug-n-Bun was featured on the Travel Channel show *Man v. Food*.

Left: Homemade root beer is something you need to try when stopping at Mug-n-Bun. *Right:* A neon sign points passersby to the parking lot of the nostalgic drive in.

It's the kind of artery-clogging food that your cardiologist warns against, but when in Rome . . . you know the rest.

A must-try when you're there, whether eating in the dining room, on the patio or in your car, is a frosty mug of their homemade root beer.

5211 W 10th St., Speedway, 317-244-5669
mug-n-bun.com

TWENTY

Restaurant in historic landmark hotel carries 1920s theme

If you want to find an eatery that is chef driven with a creative menu and an elegant and upscale vibe, you can often find it in a boutique hotel. That is the case at the Charley Creek Inn where you can experience fine dining on-site at Twenty Restaurant. Twenty is a place where you can get out for a luxurious meal and then extend the escape by making it into an overnight outing. Wake up feeling refreshed and linger before heading on your way.

The luxe accommodations in this Georgian Revival–designed hotel will transport you to a different time. The landmark debuted as Hotel Indiana in 1920 and is one of the most iconic landmarks in the county.

As is the case with many aging hotels, it went through a period of disrepair, but a local business owner and philanthropist, Richard E. Ford, was able to rescue it. He purchased the hotel and it underwent an extensive two-year renovation project to restore it to its former glory.

In 2011, the hotel was presented with the annual Outstanding Commercial Rehabilitation Award by the State of Indiana Division of Historic Preservation and Archaeology. That same year the property was also awarded the coveted Cook Cup for Outstanding Restoration (as was the historic Eagles Theatre across the street).

Once you set foot inside, you're enveloped by the glamour of the era with a grand player piano filling the lobby with lively music. Some of the rooms are named for famous Hoosiers, like the Gene Stratton Porter suite in honor of the author, nature photographer, and naturalist from Wabash County. The hotel has a total of 21 uniquely decorated guest rooms and suites.

Top left: The roaring '20s are the theme in this glamorous dining area. *Bottom Left:* Upscale entrées include a glazed salmon dish. *Center:* Old Hollywood posters and photos line the wall in this restaurant at the Charley Creek Inn. *Right:* Creative salads make for a nice start to a meal at Twenty.

Off the lobby is a charming ice cream shop and also a wine and cheese shop, a perfect place to linger and sip as you look out on downtown through the large corner windows.

Also on the first floor is the upscale dining room called Twenty with the adjacent Green Hat Lounge and some private dining rooms. Twenty has a wonderfully romantic and nostalgic ambiance. The decor harkens to a time gone by and the music sets the vibe of being out for an elegant dinner many decades ago.

Steaks, seafood, and pastas make up the bulk of the mains with some refreshing salads, comforting soups, elevated sides, and flatbreads to choose from as well. A signature cocktail, the Wabash Cannonball, is a spin on El Presidente, which was a popular drink during the decade that the Charley Creek Inn opened.

111 W Market St., Wabash, 260-563-0111
charleycreekinn.com

950 SPEAKEASY BISTRO

Family-friendly upstairs, hip hideaway downstairs in this small-town gem

There are a lot of small towns in Indiana and some that are lucky if they have one single restaurant to call their own. With no competition and a lack of foot traffic, they're sometimes average at best with nothing notable to make them a place you'd recommend.

None of that holds true for Lagro. This small community of about 400 is fortunate to have not only a cool spot for locals to hang out, but a place with impressive food and cocktails and a unique location.

950 Speakeasy Bistro opened during probably the worst time to be a restaurateur: 2020. Nevertheless, it was a hit and became a favorite of many, drawing customers from far beyond the border of this small community. It combines quality cuisine and cocktails with history, using upcycled materials in the design and construction. To be authentic to the Prohibition era, the signature cocktail list was crafted using liquors like gin and whiskey, which were prominent during that time.

Those interested in a family-friendly atmosphere where you can enjoy a pizza with the kids will be right at home in the first-level eatery. For those who are seeking something a little stronger than a soda, you can descend the staircase to a rustic speakeasy with killer craft cocktails and lovely views from the patio. The patio has a lounge area with a firepit, outdoor seating, plenty of space for socializing, and an area for live music.

Pizzas are their niche with a number of signature items offering interesting flavor combinations. A cauliflower crust option is available, or a "Riverboat" low-carb bowl can be ordered, which has of all the

Clockwise, from top left: A custom-made bar top blends well with the dark wood and exposed brick in the lower level. At the 950 Speakeasy, you enter at street level to a family friendly eatery and then make your way downstairs to the lounge that overlooks the Wabash River. A quaint patio area has seating the surrounds a fire pit. Enjoy your cocktail inside where you can look out at the Wabash River and make your way outside to the patio area. Start out your visit with a charcuterie platter of gourmet cheeses, meats, crackers, and homemade jams.

toppings mixed up in a bowl without the crust. Toasted subs, baked potatoes, salads, and small plates are part of this diverse menu of casual bites. Don't miss out on the charcuterie with a nice selection of meats, cheeses, breads, and homemade jams or spreads.

Located along the banks of the Wabash River, there's also a path for a post-dinner walk. As you explore the neighborhood, you'll spot St. Patrick's Catholic Church, founded in 1836 and placed on the National Register of Historic Places.

950 Washington St., Lagro, 260-205-8775
950speakeasy.com

A large number of Irish immigrants made their way to Lagro in the 1830s as labor for the construction of the Wabash-Erie Canal, which opened in 1943.

ONE EYED JACK'S

Home of the two-bun pork tenderloin

An accountant and an engineer with no real experience in the food industry bought a restaurant, put a breaded pork tenderloin on the menu, and the rest is history. Jenny Kasten was looking for a career change in 2014 after working as an accountant. When her friend bought a longtime diner, Vicki's Diner, and an adjoining bar, Fox's Den, she invited Kasten to work there a couple nights a week. Kasten soon realized that she loved it and convinced her husband, Mike, to buy the place. After a week of remodeling, they were in business.

The business's name came from a combination of their hobby of playing poker, the former owner of the bar "One Eyed Bob," and Mike's grandfather, Jack. The historic building in downtown Winimac is lined with wood and corrugated steel to give it a modern feel.

As a child, Kasten and her dad frequented a place that served a pork tenderloin, so they decided to put one on the menu. And that jumbo tenderloin is what they are best known for. The 12-ounce breaded tenderloin sandwich is so popular the menu has a full page dedicated to different versions of tenderloins, including The Deuce, served with two buns so that you can share. Even with two buns it still spills over the side.

They've also created a mega 7-pounder, served with 2 pounds of tater tots as a food challenge. If you're able to finish it in an hour, your meal is free and your photo goes up on the Wall of Fame. Eight professional eaters have succeeded so far.

Tenderloin lovers will also love their tenderloin bites appetizer, served with their zesty Jack Sauce. Soups are homemade daily and they offer soup flights, where you can pair three of their soups with a breadstick or a grilled cheese.

Left: If you love extreme burgers, try the Heart-O-Jack with two half-pound patties and lots of toppings. *Right:* A sign above the door of this corner building in downtown Winamac features a Jack image from a playing card.

Burgers are another popular feature, made with 8-ounce hand-patties of fresh, local Hereford beef served on toasted buns. Choose from specialty burgers, like the Heart-a-Jack Burger, which consists of two patties with a fried egg, onion ring, American, Swiss, and pepper jack cheese, bacon, barbecue sauce, two boneless chicken wings, and a mozzarella cheese stick.

Dessert is a must. Pies are made from scratch on-site, and there are four standard varieties: sugar cream, coconut cream, peanut butter, and Dutch apple, as well as seasonal and featured flavors.

There's parking outside for motorcycles or golf carts. The charming downtown is a nice setting for a little post-meal walk after you conquer your gigantic sandwich.

124 N Market St., Winamac, 574-946-4343
edinburgh-diner.wheree.com

They also run steak and seafood specials on weekends, when you can choose from a variety of beef cuts, fish, or crab entrées.

MRS. WICK'S PIES

Where you'll want to have your dessert first

When our waitress took our order, she asked if we wanted our pie or our sandwiches first. How often do you go somewhere and they ask you if you want your dessert first? But at Mrs. Wick's Pies, the dessert is that good. It's the centerpiece of the meal. There's a nice offering of sandwiches and other classic family restaurant favorites, but the pie is clearly the star of the show—and why not start with the thing that drew you there in the first place?

When we told her we'd wait and have our pie after our meal, she promised to promptly go in back and set those slices aside to ensure that they were still there for us. The pies are popular and go fast, so if your taste buds are set on a specific slice, you may want to get there early. If you want to ensure that you get exactly what you want, you can call a day or two in advance and they'll make a whole pie just for you.

This Winchester business got started in 1944 when Duane "Wick" Wickersham was a delivery driver. One day while making his delivery, he overheard a manager talking about an accident that had been caused by an employee who had gone to a pub and gotten intoxicated on his lunch break. It turned out it was a common problem. Wick suggested they open a café in the factory where employees could stay on premises and have something to eat. The next week the owners asked him if he'd like to start a cantina in the building and he was in business.

After a year, he left and started the Rainbow Restaurant in downtown Winchester. Many of his grandmother's recipes were used in the restaurant, including homemade pies. The pies were so popular that he started delivering them out of his 1934 Buick sedan, setting a goal of selling 300 pies per day, which he met in the first four years.

Business continued to boom, and he knew he would need a bigger place to bake. In 1961, he bought a building for his new production line

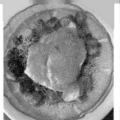

Left to right: Fruit pies with crumb topping are just one of the varieties you'll find here. If you're in the mood for breakfast with your pie, try one of their skillets. When you buy a pie to go, it comes in a sturdy box with an image of Mrs. Wick on it. The bakery and cafe draw people from all over to sit and have a meal or get pies to go.

that allowed for shipment of frozen pies. Today, they produce 10,000 pies and more than 30,000 pie shells in an eight-hour shift.

When Wick retired from the pie business in 1986, he opened a restaurant in honor of his wife, Ruby. Mrs. Wick's Restaurant is a full-service bakery café and retail outlet where you can buy fresh pies or shop from the freezer inventory of unbaked frozen pies, pot pies, noodles, and pie shells. You can also order pies for direct shipping on the restaurant's website.

The business is a family affair with their children and now grandchildren involved in the business. The company employs more than 70 additional employees as part of the Wick's Pies family.

Several of the pies are award winners, but the pie that started it all way back when Wick started making pies from his grandma's recipes was the sugar cream pie, which has since been designated as the official Indiana state pie.

The Wick's version of this Hoosier delicacy contains high-quality cream, sugar, and nutmeg among its ingredients. When eggs were sold out on the farm, they were omitted from the pie, and that's how it's made today—without eggs. It's described as similar in taste to crème brûlée.

100 N Cherry St., Winchester, 765-584-7437
wickspies.com

Get an incredibly affordable meal here. With the exception of whole pies, you won't find anything on the menu over $10.

CAMMACK STATION

"Cammack and see us"

Cammack (pronounced kuh-mack) is a little community in Delaware County between Yorktown and Muncie. It was founded as a sawmill town in 1882. From the 1930s on, a little store and filling station served the community. It had various owners over the years, but most recently it was called Pete's Grocery. It was packed to the gills, had gas pumps outside, and Pete prepared a couple things on his little grill for hungry customers: fried bologna and his onion burger.

Today, this little unincorporated community has an attraction that draws in scores of people from around the world. Pete's is now Cammack Station, a restaurant that doubles as a museum of fun, nostalgic memorabilia. A recent addition doubled the size of the eatery and allowed for much more space to display the growing collection of 1940s-, '50s-, and '60s-era gas pumps, signs, statues, jukeboxes, and more that covers walls (and ceilings) inside and outside.

Among the collection are statues of Mickey Mantle and Marilyn Monroe, a guitar that belonged to Elvis, a jukebox belonging to Garfield creator Jim Davis loaded with 45s that he listened to as he drew the comic strip, and signed photos of the cast of *The Andy Griffith Show* (which was Pete's favorite television show).

Each Monday when the restaurant is closed, manager Shane Shafer adds a few more items to the decor. So, if you visit and then go back a week later, there will be new pieces to look for. About 95 percent of what you'll find there are genuine antiques.

In 2015, there were fewer than 30 seats in the restaurant. Now there are 168. Future plans include a kitchen expansion, restoration of a grainery, and more. Big crowds come out for the car shows and cruise-ins from April through October. Proceeds from these events go to local charities.

Clockwise, from top left: The former gas station turned eatery/museum has a nostalgic facade with antique gas pumps and signs. A juke box in the dining room once belonged to local success story, Jim Davis, who created the cartoon *Garfield*. It is full of songs he played as he worked on sketches. Filled with authentic vintage signs and memorabilia, the dining room doubles as a museum. There are two dozen ice cream flavors to choose from, including Hoosier sugar cream pie. Bacon-wrapped hot dogs are a popular menu item. In honor of the former gas station that made fried bologna sandwiches for customers, Cammack Station has a fried bologna sandwich on the menu. The bologna is house-made and you get about five thick slices placed on a bun.

On the menu are items using local beef and pork, locally grown vegetables, and locally made Sundaes Ice Cream in the 18 to 36 percent butterfat range. Bologna for the fried bologna sandwiches that were a staple at Pete's is made in-house. Shortcakes and brownies are baked from scratch. Strawberries are hand sliced.

The side that housed the original gas station has an ice cream counter where you can select from 24 flavors of ice cream with unique flavors like Hoosier sugar cream pie and Graham Cammack Station, which has chunks of graham crackers in vanilla ice cream. The seasonal strawberry shortcake is a much-anticipated treat—between March and September last year, they sold 11,000 servings of it.

9200 W Jackson St., Muncie, 765-759-3871
cammackstation.com

Things get very busy here during the travel season, but you can make reservations ahead to be sure you get a table when you arrive.

JOHN'S FAMOUS STEW

Go for the stew, stay for the cobbler

John's Famous Stew is definitely off the beaten path. It sits as a lone restaurant in an industrial area where blue-collar workers—construction crews, cops, transportation workers—make up much of their customer base. There are also local regulars and out-of-towners who go there to be reminded of a taste of home.

The restaurant has existed since 1911, but its recipes date back even earlier. They came from Dapa Strangeff, who cooked stew in iron kettles on wood-burning stoves for her family of nine children in Macedonia in the 1800s. Two of her sons settled in Indianapolis in 1911 and started the restaurant, making the stew from the recipe of Mother Strangeff, who lived to be 99 years old. The same recipe from the old country is still how the stew is made today. The restaurant has been in the current building since 1975.

That famous stew is a hearty dish of big beef chunks in a savory beef broth with potatoes and carrots. Alongside it come slices of white bread. You can select your heat level: mild, "medium with a touch of heat," or "hot, very spicy." Go even further and ask for hot peppers to be added. You may also want to try John's Stew Burger, a third-pounder with a big scoop of stew poured on top. Almost as famous as the stew is John's Famous Tenderloin Supreme—a giant breaded pork loin smothered in stew. The Hot Minced Pie is a hot stew with butter beans and hot peppers added. There's also a Goulash Stew with butter

Indiana native David Letterman is one of the famous names to have eaten at John's Famous Stew.

Left: Sit at the bar and have a beer or cocktail with your stew or sandwich. *Top left:* The simple nondescript facade of John's Stew sits a little off the beaten path in an industrial area. *Top right:* Cups of John's Famous Stew are served with white bread and can be customized to your desired spice level. *Bottom right:* The no-frills dining room has plenty of seating for hungry crowds.

beans and garden vegetables blended in. The Stuffed Pepper Stew has a fresh green pepper loaded with rice covered in stew. Also on the menu is Stew & Smashed Potatoes, which is a big bowl loaded with hot smashed potatoes and stew topping.

And while it was the stew recipe that the restaurant was founded on, there is way, way more than just stew to get your fill of when you're there. Other comfort specialties include a cabbage roll that comes topped with stew gravy, chili, a beef or turkey Manhattan, country fried steak, a Reuben sandwich, and more.

No meal at John's Famous Stew is complete without a piece of the homemade cobbler, which can be one of a few different fruit flavors: peach, blackberry, cherry, or apple. It sells out quickly, so be sure to get there early in the day before it's gone. And there's a beverage you don't often see on restaurant menus that you can order to accompany your cobbler: a glass of cold buttermilk.

1146 Kentucky Ave., Indianapolis, 317-636-6212

BAO'S PASTRY

A taste of France in Northwest Indiana

After living in France for 10 years, Bao Ngoc and her family decided to make the move to the United States, bringing with her a passion for pastries and a desire to bring them to the Valparaiso community.

Born in Vietnam, Bao moved to Paris after college, where she trained as a pastry chef and graduated with a professional pastry degree from the Auguste Escoffier School of Culinary Arts. She began working at bakeries and pastry boutiques around Paris.

After arriving in the United States in 2018, she began working as a vendor at local markets where her pastries were so wildly popular that she quickly grew a customer base to support a brick-and-mortar store. Her French pastry shop opened in 2020, where she wowed customers with colorful works of food art.

The desserts are feasts for the eyes: colorful French macaroons; Napoleons with layers of puff pastry and artistic icing patterns; and tarts topped with fresh, glazed fruits.

On any given day you'll find such beautiful sweet indulgences as crème brûlée, Parisian flan, pain au chocolate, cream puffs, and madelines. Croissants come in many flavors, among them raspberry creme, cinnamon, Nutella, pistachio chocolate, and ham apple brie.

A large variety of puff pastries and tarts are on display, made from the finest ingredients and with traditional Parisan cooking techniques. Cakes are nothing short of masterpieces, from the lemon layer cake to

A second location at 607 E Lincolnway is in the works in a historic Valparaiso house that will include a tearoom, larger baking facilities, and a classroom space for workshops.

Top left: You'll find extreme attention to detail in every dessert. *Top right:* A group participates in a pastry-making workshop. *Center left:* Lemon Lavender is a seasonal cake that is a customer favorite. *Center right:* Individual cake slices are available every day. *Bottom:* Macarons are a classic French treat that you can indulge in at Bao's.

opera cake to strawberry diplomat. You can also order macaron towers in lieu of cake for special occasions. And if you're looking for less sweet and more savory bites, you'll want to try the quiche.

Even more treats can be found for special holidays like Thanksgiving, Christmas, and Easter, including Bûches de Noël, carrot cakes, hot cross buns, and handcrafted salted caramel-filled hens. Also, look for seasonal specialties like the blueberry lemon cake. During festival and market season, you'll also find Bao's booth at area markets and events.

12 Jefferson St., Valparaiso, 219-299-8693
baopastry.com

ROCK-COLA CAFE

Classic American 1950s diner bringing back popular '50s beverage

Ah, the 1950s. It was a decade defined by rock 'n' roll, big snazzy cars in pastel hues, teenage heartthrobs, jukeboxes, optimism, and postwar prosperity. When you look back at American history, there are few decades more idealized than the 1950s.

Iconic images of the era evoke a sense of euphoric times. Suburban development. Poodle skirts and saddle shoes. Drive-in movie theaters. Sock hops. Elvis Presley.

The Rock-Cola Cafe in Indianapolis captures the essence of the '50s perfectly in this nostalgic diner with black and white checkered tile, vinyl-covered booths and barstools, a jukebox, and vintage signs.

Two high school friends joined together to open this happy place, and the diners continue to pour in for this blast from the past. One also took it a step further, bringing back an Indiana beverage that was popular throughout the '50s: Choc-Ola.

Formulated by former restaurant and ice cream entrepreneur Harry Normington Sr. in 1944, Choc-Ola was originally manufactured on the south side of Indianapolis and later acquired by the Chocolate Group, parent company of Yoo-Hoo, another popular chocolate drink. Around 2003, production stopped.

In 2009, owner Dan Iaria embarked on a mission to revive the tradition of making this nostalgic drink in Indianapolis, and you can now enjoy a cold glass with your meal at Rock-Cola.

The menu has the classics you'd expect from a diner of that era. Fresh, juicy burgers; crunchy fries; creamy homemade milkshakes. But there's a lot more to choose from among the breakfast, lunch,

Clockwise, from top left: Fun nostalgic items can be found throughout the diner, like a rotary phone. Freshly-made loaded burgers are a customer favorite. The sign outside indicates that Rock Cola Cafe is the new home of Choc-Ola Chocolate Drink. Walking in the door is an instant throwback to the 1950s.

and dinner menus. The Mile High Club sandwich is a variation on a classic club using Texas toast held together by a knife rather than toothpicks. The Mr. Big Stuff is their breakfast-lunch hybrid with a grilled burger patty topped with two fried eggs and thick slices of hickory-smoked bacon. The Trailer Park is a giant hash brown patty topped with scrambled eggs, ham, green pepper, onion, and American cheese.

The menu is large with more diner food and unique items, from Reubens to the cajun burger to steak to grilled tenderloins.

5730 S Brookville Rd., Indianapolis, 317-357-2233

IECHYD DA BREWING COMPANY

Mom-and-pop place focuses on session beers, casual grub with Welsh influence

Chip Lewis has always been drawn to his Welsh heritage. The family has traced it back to the 1600s, when the first in the Lewis line immigrated to the US. That influence can be found throughout Iechyd Da's name to the logo to some of the beer styles.

Chip and his wife, Summer, had been home-brewing for several years before they made the leap to build a brewery on Main Street in their hometown. The result is a mom-and-pop operation where everyone feels welcome, whether bellied up to the bar, enjoying the warmth of the sun on the patio, or seated along the row of tables that are so close it's almost like a beer-hall environment where you can't help but strike up a conversation with your neighbors.

The whole place is one that encourages connection and community and the simple pleasure of hanging out with people you love or meeting new people and doing nothing but enjoying a beer.

Brews trend toward the sessionable with mild English ales and lagers, but you'll find a nice variety of other styles in their 10 on-tap options. You'll find only their beers, but they do have some guest wines, ciders, and slushies. Names of the beers often refer to a bit of

> Get a sitter or drop the kids off at Grandma's. Iechyd Da is a 21 and over pub.

Clockwise, from top left: Besides table seating, there are comfortable lounge chairs, as well. Iechyd Da Brewing sits along Main Street in Elkhart and has outdoor dining in the warmer months. Choose a flight and try 5-ounce pours of several different brews. Pizza is a mainstay on the menu with a few standard specialty varieties, but you can also customize your toppings or try their monthly special.

Welsh history or family or personal history. Some are named after cities in Wales or one of the 600 castles in the Welsh countryside, like Kidwelly, which dates back to the 1200s. Also, the image that makes up the brewery's logo comes from Chip's family crest.

Aside from beer, this brewpub serves up some pretty spectacular food and is known for their house pizzas, which go way beyond sauce and mozzarella cheese, using goat cheese, artichoke hearts, shaved Pecorino cheese, local bacon, smoked gouda, sundried tomatoes, and arugula among ingredients. You'll always find one or two limited-time concoctions on the menu, too, so be sure to get those while you can.

And if you're wondering how the heck to pronounce the name of this place, you're not alone. Few people get it right on the first try. Yah-key-Dah. Now say it fast three times. It's a Welsh toast that translates to "good health." It's just another way to say Cheers!, Salud, or Prost!

317 N Main St., Elkhart, 574-293-0506
iechyddabrewingcompany.com

THE FARMHOUSE RESTAURANT AT FAIR OAKS FARMS

The ultimate farm-to-table experience

Fair Oaks Farms is a destination that is a working farm with the mission of welcoming guests to experience joy and enrichment through reconnecting with the land, nurturing body and soul, and being immersed in innovate efforts to sustainably feed our world.

It's a perfect place for family outings or school field trips with educational components and hands-on play that give an overview of farming along with fun and enlightening activities. You could easily spend a full day there, or with a hotel on-site, you could make it into a fun-filled overnighter or weekend getaway.

There are experiential museums, adventures, and tours that allow visitors to take in the wonder of modern dairy farming, learn about raising pigs, and see the scope of agriculture's role in feeding the world.

Along with hands-on exhibits, there are also play areas that encourage physical activity, like an indoor ropes course and a big inflatable bouncing area. During the harvest season, you can wander the U-pick orchards and fields to select apples, sunflowers, and pumpkins.

The Farmhouse Restaurant is a true farm-to-fork experience. Not only does it produce dishes with ingredients that are farm fresh, but it's part of the farm where the ingredients are grown. After exploring family-owned farms, you can have a meal that is as fresh as it gets, with produce grown just outside the restaurants and meat raised on-site.

Left: The Farmhouse Restaurant is part of the Fair Oaks Farms complex, which includes interactive exhibits, a U-pick orchard, ice cream parlor, hotel and more. *Right:* Fresh farm-to-table dishes and hearty comfort food are among the menu selections.

Recognized as the number one agritourism destination in the Midwest, it's also located right in the corn belts of Northwest Indiana, where fertile soil yields excellent produce.

The freshness is evident in each bite, from the stone-fired artisan pizzas to the enticing salads and comforting entrées, such as fried chicken, bacon-wrapped meat loaf, and chicken pot pie. Certified Angus beef cuts and pork chops are the centerpiece of the menu with scratch-made sides.

If you're short on time, stop in the Cowfé for a quicker meal. The grilled cheese promises to be some of the best you'll ever have.

754 N 600 E, Fair Oaks, 219-394-3663
fofarms.com

Stop in the deli for foodie souvenirs like award-winning cheese and milk bottled at the farm.

SCHNITZELBANK

A bit of Germany in Southern Indiana

Once in a while you find an eatery that takes you to a completely different place. You don't simply go there to get food in your belly. You go there for the cultural experience and to learn a little about a place far away. By making your way to the historically German community of Jasper, you are taken a world away for hearty Bavarian recipes and a stein of frosty beer.

Since 1961, Schnitzelbank has been transporting diners to Germany in their little corner of Southern Indiana. Owners Larry and Betty Hanselman enjoy inviting guests into their world and into their family. It started with a tavern that was purchased in 1961, but the family wanted to expand their offerings and create a true haven where German recipes and culture could be fully appreciated. The old tavern was torn down in 1971 and replaced with a new building, and Schnitzelbank was born.

Not only will you leave feeling satisfied by generous portions of stick-to-your-ribs food, but you won't be able to make it out the door without learning at least one German word. Gemütlichkeit! Glockenspiel. Sauerbraten. You may even leave speaking an accent the likes of Arnold Schwarzenegger.

The destination restaurant has ranked in the top 10 independent restaurants in the state. Before you make it inside, you'll already be feeling the vibes of Deutschland. The authentic working glockenspiel is an animated mechanical clock similar to, although much smaller in scale, ones you'll find in places like Munich and other cities throughout the country. At designated times, it plays tunes on a number of bells and instruments. (At time of publication, the glockenspiel was in the process of being repaired.)

The old-world ambiance extends inside, where you know you're not in Kansas anymore. On the walls, behind the bar, even in the

Left: Enjoy a German feast with the German Sample Platter, which comes with eight meats and five sides. *Center:* Waitresses come to your table dressed in traditional dirndls. *Right:* You'll find several German imported beers on draft in sizes from 10 ounces up to a 64-ounce boot.

tablecloths are signs of German traditions. Waitresses serve you dressed in traditional garb called dirndls. The ambiance, food quality, and good service make it Der platz fuer speise, trunk, und gemuetlichkeit! Or The place for food, drink, and good cheer!

Dubbed the "Wunderbar," their sizable soup and salad bar will allow you to sample several German and American salads, vegetables, fruits, and two soup choices each day.

They're known throughout the Midwest for their authentic German cuisine specialties—or Deutsche spezialitäten. From schnitzel to sauerbraten to sausages, the meat lovers will be happy when they peruse the menu. There's plenty of American fare, too, if heavy German food isn't your jam.

Try some traditional potato pancakes, which are a great start to the meal. Spaetzle, hot German potato salad, and red cabbage are traditional sides that you have to try. And on Fridays, you can enjoy a hearty all-you-can-eat fish fry. There are so many choices, you'll leave as happy as a two-fisted, stein-holding tuba player in an oompah band.

The beer is always flowing, and you can sip or chug a heavy stein of on-draft imports as you shout, "Prost!"

393 3rd Ave., Jasper, 812-482-2640
schnitzelbank.com

Don't leave without stopping in the gift shop for an assortment of classic German items like nutcrackers, shot glasses, apparel, advent calendars, and ornaments.

IOZZO'S GARDEN OF ITALY

Old-world charm and family recipes are a winning combination

If you're looking for a spot for authentic Italian cuisine where just about everything is house made, then make your way to Iozzo's Garden of Italy. The Iozzo family arrived in America from their native Calabria, Italy, in the early 1900s and brought with them recipes and traditions of previous generations. Santoro "Fred" Iozzo and his new bride, Rosaria "Rosa," first settled in Boston and Ohio where he worked on the railroads. They moved their way west to Indianapolis, where he got started in the grocery business. In just a few years, it had grown to a 21-grocery store empire.

The Great Depression hit the business hard, and the chain shut down. In 1930, Fred began utilizing the culinary skills he had learned in Italy to open Naples Grill, the first full-service Italian restaurant in Indianapolis. The restaurant later moved and expanded to become one of the largest restaurants in the Midwest, with three bars, a banquet room, two kitchens, and a bandstand. It was renamed Iozzo's Garden of Italy.

In 1940, the restaurant closed after an unfortunate shooting that occurred in the restaurant. Fred died in 1944 and with him died the family's involvement in serving Italian cuisine. But in 2009, the Iozzo traditions were revived by Fred's great-granddaughter, Katie Harris, when she opened Iozzo's Garden of Italy on Meridian Street. After 15 years, the restaurant is going strong with plans for expansion of another location in the near future. It's won awards from different publications for "Best New Restaurant" and "Best Italian Restaurant in Indianapolis."

One must-try is Iozzo's hand-rolled meatballs made with a blend of veal, pork, and beef that is slow cooked in sauce for about seven hours.

Left: Iozzo's reopened in 2009, with the owner continuing the legacy of her grandfather and great-grandfather who once operated a restaurant in Indianapolis. *Right:* A nice filet can be added to your order of gnocchi.

You can order them as a "meatball martini" appetizer in a large martini glass with a scoop of spaghetti settled on the bottom. The lasagna bolognese is a definite standout as well, with five filled layers covered in half bolognese and half alfredo sauce and served in cast iron.

With fine Italian dining, there must be wine. And there is definitely an abundance of wine to be poured. There's an extensive list of Italian reds from such places as Tuscany, Calabria, Sicily, and Piedmont as well as a list of primarily California reds. The majority of white wines and sparkling wines are from Italy with a sampling from California, France, and New Zealand. You can also pick up a bottle of the Heritage Wine Collection, a private-label red created for Iozzo's in Paso Robles, California.

The beer list includes a few Midwest craft brews, and a significant signature cocktail list gives you an opportunity to try something fresh.

All desserts except gelato are made on-site, and their selections are beyond scrumptious: tiramisu cheesecake, chocolate pudding, cannoli, and ricotta zeppole.

946 S Meridian St., Indianapolis, 317-974-1100
iozzos.com

In the warmer months, settle yourself outside on the patio, where you won't feel like you're near a bustling interstate but a world away.

THE PORT DRIVE-IN

Why drive through when you can drive in?

The 1950s was an era of good times. And a lot of those good times were had at diners and drive-ins where you could hang out with friends and enjoy some burgers and shakes with some toe-tapping rock 'n' roll tunes. If you went the route of taking your vehicle to a drive-in, you could enjoy your meal from the spacious bench seat in your land yacht of a car with a tray hanging from your partially rolled-down window, delivered by a friendly carhop.

Since 1953, that's been the day-to-day at the Port Drive-In. And you can still have the experience of those cool cats of earlier decades. Pull up in your car, give your order to a live person, have it brought to your window, and do some dashboard dining.

Originally called Studeman's, it was purchased by Elsie & Virgil Gassoway in 1957 and renamed the Snack Shack and later The Port. In 1978, Terry and Beth Gassoway purchased the business from Terry's parents after managing it for several years. It was later sold to Zig and Iris Skrzypczak, who run it now with their children, keeping the same traditions and original recipes that have kept it a beloved landmark in the Indiana Dunes community of Chesterton.

The menu started simple but has expanded over the years. It currently includes more than 100 items. And while there are lots of delicious items to choose from, you need to start out with the full nostalgic experience of getting a frosted mug of their root beer, which is still made on the premises, and a chili dog, which is still made using Elsie's original recipes.

Left: The Port Drive-In in Chesterton has been serving customers from their cars since 1953.
Right: Make sure you try the homemade root beer.

Once you've eased in with these signature items, go ahead and go wild. Try a giant, half-pound hot dog; a bacon-wrapped L.A. Street Dog; a burger topped with grilled jalapeños and onion, cheese, jalapeño poppers, onion rings, and Thai chili mayo called the Anchor; or their giant pork tenderloin.

They also offer fried clams, fish and shrimp, chicken tenders, tacos, pizza puffs, BLTs, toasted cheese, Italian beef, grilled ham and cheese, and more. Beyond burgers and black bean burgers are available for the non-meat eaters.

In addition to their homemade root beer, you can wash down your meal with a root beer float, a milkshake, or a Green River.

419 N Calumet Rd., Chesterton, 219-926-3500
theportdrivein.net

Dining in your car isn't required. There are also picnic tables and an air-conditioned dining room.

MACRI'S ITALIAN BAKERY & TRATTORIA AND CARMELA'S AT MACRI'S

Get the best of Italian cuisine and baked goods in one trip

Macri's Italian Bakery is the place that sweet dreams are made of. When Annie Lennox sang of sweet dreams, she could have very well been talking about this South Bend haven of everything sugary.

It all started with the sweet dream of an Italian couple who came to America and decided to share the beloved food of their homeland. George and Iole opened the doors to Macri's Italian Bakery in 1978 on LaSalle Avenue, next to the Macris' other family business, Macri's Jewelry. Fifteen years later, it relocated to its current location where it's been a Michiana staple ever since. It has expanded to include a full-service trattoria.

You'll be hit with a million tantalizing scents as you walk in the doors, and your eyes will widen as you scan the cases of cookies, muffins, cupcakes, pastries, kolachky, cheesecake, and Italian specialties like biscotti and cannoli. They also make stunning custom cakes.

On the trattoria side, you can select a hand-pressed panini, signature wood-fired pizza, salad, or pasta. If you're looking for something quick and casual, this is a perfect spot.

If you'd like to sit down to a more formal dinner experience, you can do that now thanks to a second generation of Macris.

Son George Jr. grew up in the bakery kitchen working alongside his parents, and when he married Carmela, it was a match made in foodie

Left: A classic chicken parmesan is a perfect meal to enjoy when dining at Carmela's at Macri's. *Right:* The patio area provides a nice outdoor seating space. *Left center:* Mozzarella sticks are one of the signature menu items, which are made fresh in-house. *Bottom left:* Don't pass up dessert when you visit. Each item is made from scratch in the adjoining bakery space of Macri's Italian Bakery & Trattoria.

heaven. Carmela is an accomplished cook who learned her skills from her mother and mother-in-law, and she's the brilliance behind the cakes at Macri's Bakery and most of the signature dishes at Carmela's, the Italian fine-dining spot located right next door. The couple are continuing the Macri family traditions running the businesses along with their four children.

Carmela's has an upscale ambiance and attentive service with authentic Italian cuisine in generous portions. Pasta dishes are made in-house, with such entrées as lobster ravioli, gamberi carbonara, linguine Bolognese meatballs and baked cheese tortellini. Hearty portions of beef, pork, chicken and fish are inspired by flavors of Italy.

214 N Niles Ave., South Bend, 574-282-1010 and 574-280-4824

THE TACO DIVE

Southeast Chicago Mexican Inn's recipes resurrected at beach "dive bar"

The Taco Dive is a fairly new restaurant, having opened in Whiting in 2019, but its story began decades earlier. Owner David Jimenez is carrying on family traditions in a modern, chill space with beloved recipes that have been feeding those in the region for over 60 years.

Jimenez is the nephew of Mario Cornejo Sr., who opened the famed Mexican Inn on Chicago's Southeast Side in 1961. The place did a booming business with customers waiting in lines outside on weekends to get a taste of Cornejo's dishes, which were a mix of Mexican and Tex-Mex styles.

Jimenez learned how to make his uncle's recipes, and after his uncle passed away, he decided to continue the legacy by opening a restaurant and sharing those much-beloved dishes. For a few years, he was in business in Dyer with a place called Taco Trader that closed in 2016.

After a little time off, he decided to do some pop-ups in Whiting, where he resided. A local restaurant and then the American Legion post invited him in to do pop-ups, so he could gauge the interest. They were an instant hit. When he began the pop-ups, he was selling out in less than an hour. After those successful runs, he found an available building on the main street through downtown that he thought would be a good fit. Before long, The Taco Dive was born.

The space is not just a place to drop in and pick up food. It's reminiscent of a breezy beach bar where all your cares are gone once you walk through the door. It proudly calls itself a "hole-in-the-wall," and you definitely feel vacation vibes as you sit at a table with water-colored walls adorned with giant swordfish and surfboards.

Left: The cripsy beef tacos were a popluar signature item at The Mexican Inn in Chicago that you can now find at The Taco Dive. *Center:* The interior of Taco Dive gives the feel of a relaxing beach bar. *Right:* Owner David Jimenez has recreated recipes that his uncle, Mario Cornejo Sr., served when he owned the Mexican Inn on Chicago's Southeast Side. Credit The Taco Dive

Situated just down the road from Lake Michigan's Whihala Beach, it's a place where you can spend a day in the sun, shake off the sand, and come inside to continue the beach vibe.

The popular trademark crispy tacos and "It's a 95th and Ewing thing" soft cheese are the bestsellers and must-try items. The crispy tacos are done the same way Uncle Mario made them. They're pinned by hand with toothpicks before they're fried. You can get them filled with beef, chicken, or beans. The soft cheese is a cheese-filled corn tortilla rolled and smothered in a rich, creamy cheese sauce that is more like cheesy béchamel than a queso. You can also get those filled with your meat of choice or beans.

The beans and rice are also old family recipes. And there are a few menu items created by Jimenez that have his own spin: a Sonoran hot dog and a sloppy Jose, which is a loose-leaf sandwich on soft Mexican bread sourced from a south-side bakery. Premium meat is bought locally from Howard & Sons meats in Munster, and tortillas come from Chicago's Pilsen neighborhood. Quality and supporting local businesses are of utmost importance to Jimenez.

1452 119th St., Whiting, 219-614-6289
thetacodive.com

MISHKENUT MEDITERRANEAN CUISINE

Offering flavors of Italy and the Middle East

At Mishkenut, chef Abe Hinnawi recognizes that food can unite people, and that has been his objective since opening this little kitchen in the far northwest corner of the state. The idea of opening his own restaurant remained an obsession through his youth and young adulthood.

He was introduced to food hospitality while working with his uncle at a renowned restaurant in West Jerusalem in 1975 that was a well-visited spot among local celebrities and government officials.

After years of practicing his craft and perfecting his dishes, he has brought his skills and passion for sharing the flavors of his homeland to Mishkenut Mediterranean Cuisine. From his filet mignon dipped in dijon mustard sauce to his veal mandolin smothered in a cream-and-mushroom sauce to his devola chicken, Abe's talent is on full display in the colorfully plated dishes and his Middle Eastern specialties like hummus, falafel, and shish kebab.

The foundation of Mediterranean cooking is freshness with a big focus on seafood, vegetables, plant-based proteins, and healthy oils. A Mediterranean diet is often recommended for improved heart health for its emphasis on fresh vegetables and fruits, whole grains, extra virgin olive oil, nuts, legumes, and fish. It's light on red meats, heavy on beans, scarce on sweets, limited on cheese and dairy, and absent of processed foods.

The dining room is small, as is the kitchen. The staff of family members is small, so keep that in mind and be patient if you have to wait a little bit for a table or your meal. This is one to sit and savor

Ordering a combination platter is a good way to get an overview of Mediterranean food and sample smaller portions of several different dishes.

rather than gulp down and be on your way. They also do a brisk carryout business, and there's always the option of ordering ahead and taking food to go if you're pressed on time. The restaurant is a modest little spot inside a strip mall along busy Ridge Road, wedged between a nostalgic hamburger joint and a barber shop.

If you have a hard time deciding on what to select, the kebob plate lunch combo is a good way to go. It gives a nice overview of Mediterranean cooking, including chicken, kufta, beef, and falafel with rice, salad, hummus, and pita bread.

221 Ridge Rd., Munster, 219-836-6069
mishkenut.com

Family members return to their land in Jerusalem to harvest olives and press their own olive oil. Ask if they have any bottles available for purchase while you're there.

THE WORKINGMAN'S FRIEND

Smash burgers are the star at this low-key, no-frills tavern

What's been called the "Best Burger in the State" by *Food & Wine Magazine* is made in a modest little west-side tavern that hasn't changed much over time. The spot was established as Belmont Lunch in 1918 by a Macedonian man, 19-year-old Louis Stamatkin, whose family immigrated to the US when he was a child.

Originally, it catered to local railroad workers, and Stamatkin earned the nickname "The Working Man's Friend" after he would let customers accumulate IOUs during a strike in 1922. When his sons took over the business in the 1940s following his death, they renamed the place Working Man's Friend in his honor. It was later shortened to two words: Workingman's Friend.

His sons sought to take things up a notch, and it worked in the prosperous postwar years. They expanded the beverage menu from beer to a lengthy cocktail menu with martinis, old fashioneds, screwdrivers, Tom Collinses, Bloody Marys, Singapore slings, sweet after-dinner drinks, and more. They also added 18-ounce T-bone steaks to the menu and had white tablecloths and air conditioning, a luxury at the time. Live music was brought in, and some early acts on their stage went on to have impressive music careers.

In the late 1970s, Stamatkin's granddaughter, Becky Stamatkin, started working there in her early teens, and she's still there today. It's returned to its roots of simple food and concentrates more on beer. It still serves the workingman as it did in the beginning.

It's a work boots and sneakers type of establishment with old-school, well-aged linoleum tile, formica tables with red leather chairs, defunct cigarette vending machines, and the feel of a 1950s diner. But it's also common to see a customer in a suit or a millennial in skinny jeans

Left: Becky Stamatkin, granddaughter of the founder of The Workingman's Friend, started working at the restaurant as a teenager in the 1970s and operates the eatery today. *Right:* The bright bar area serves up drinks along with their simple menu.

noshing on a burger and fries. You'll find workers in for a quick lunch break and mature retirees sitting back for a long conversation over lunch. It's really an any-man's diner more than a workingman's place these days.

It does have workingman prices. It has a brief menu, posted on boards in the dining room. One abbreviated menu gives prices for the most popular items: the giant double cheeseburger, french fries, homemade chili, and beer-battered onion rings. While the burger, a crispy yet juicy smash burger, is what people flock there for, there are about a dozen sandwich options, from a hot ham and cheese on rye to smoked sausage to braunschweiger. Sides range from fried mushrooms to bean soup to sweet potato fries to tater tots.

The pork tenderloin is a notable item that is cut fresh and hand breaded.

Things move fast inside. Servers show up quickly. Your food arrives in a flash. It's portable stuff that doesn't require a fork and knife. It's easy grub that the workingman can consume quickly before he has to get back to finish a shift.

Hours are limited, from just 11 a.m. to 2:45 p.m., Tuesday through Saturday, with later hours on just one night: they stay open on Friday until 8 p.m. Also, be sure to stop at the bank or ATM before visiting. It's a cash-only business.

234 N Belmont Ave., Indianapolis, 317-636-2067

> **One of the rare, sacred places that is just for grown-ups, this burger joint is for those age 21 and older.**

121

DESSERTS BY JULIETTE

Bakery born from a blog and a buttercream recipe

In 2018, Susan Keller and her daughter, Juliette, started a blog when they were facing the difficulty of caring for Susan's mother as her health was declining. Juliette was her grandmother's primary caregiver during the day, and Susan and her husband, Daryle, cared for her at night.

Susan and Juliette had taken cake decorating classes together in the past and came from a long line of home bakers. Juliette passed the time baking while she was with her grandmother, pulling from those skills she'd learned.

The two decided to start sharing the experience on a blog. Susan would take photos of her creations in the evening and Juliette would share recipes. The three generations had some good bonding time over food.

The blog took off, and one post in particular got a lot of attention. A recipe for Italian chocolate buttercream ended up ranking at the top of Google searches, and they wondered if there might be a market for it. They didn't know of anywhere locally where you could get Italian buttercream. They started creating small batches out of a local commercial kitchen and selling them at local markets, where they often sold out.

Soon those customers who were buying the icing were making requests for custom cakes, and their side hustle grew. Eventually, they got so busy they knew it was time to venture out and open their own place.

When a spot opened in downtown Kouts, they launched their bakery serving treats using that popular Italian buttercream icing

Left: After starting out selling at local markets, the bakery is now a full-time job for Susan and Daryle Keller. *Center:* Decorative cupcakes can be found in the cooler during regular hours. *Right:* This bakery in Kouts was the result of a food blog started by a mother and daughter in 2018.

as well as other indulgent sweets. Today, you can still order custom cakes as well as select ready-to-go baked goods in the cases, including cupcakes, doughnuts, scones, cookies, cakes, cake pops, hot chocolate bombs, and other goodies. There's also a selection of fancy coffee drinks to pair with your dessert.

Susan and Daryle now operate the bakery full time. They also prepare some fun seasonal flavors and varieties, like strawberry shortcake, shamrock pistachio cake, and pumpkin patch cakes. Each month they have a seasonal feature, and they have a Cake of the Month subscription where you're guaranteed one of the featured cakes at a discount by prepaying.

As the business has grown, they've expanded to supply desserts for area restaurants and create elaborate wedding cakes. They also have keto-friendly and gluten-free desserts available.

As for that Italian buttercream, it is a little more time consuming than making traditional buttercream, but to the Kellers, it's worth that extra effort. It's got a light, silky consistency, is less sweet than traditional buttercream, and is shelf stable. You can still buy it in a 16-ounce tub in the store.

401 S Main St., Kouts, 219-299-5824
dessertsbyjuliette.com

BALLARD'S IN THE ATRIUM

Dine in the atrium of the "Eighth Wonder of the World"

When the West Baden Springs Hotel opened in 1902, it was dubbed the "Eighth Wonder of the World" due to its massive freestanding dome, which was the largest in the world at that time. The hotel was visited by the rich and famous from around the country who made their way to the area for the healing properties of the mineral water. It continued entertaining the wealthy and well-connected until 1932. Like many businesses of that era, it couldn't survive the affects of the Great Depression.

For decades it served as a Jesuit College and had other uses before sitting abandoned in the late 1900s. A huge renovation project took place, returning the hotel to its former glory and reopening in 2006. The atrium is the centerpiece of the property and in one corner of the interior is a seating area called Ballard's in the Atrium.

The eatery offers casual dining with an upscale twist. Food options include appetizers, salads, pizza, and sandwiches, but you can also enjoy seafood or steak. Whatever you choose, your dining experience includes a breathtaking backdrop of the dome, statues and balconies and an atmosphere like no other. The atrium also features a huge, decorative fireplace that is large enough to fit a 14-foot log. A grand piano sits in the atrium and is often played during dinner hours, adding to the luxurious ambiance.

The restaurant and adjacent Ballard's Bar are named for Ed Ballard, who owned West Baden Springs Hotel during its heyday in the 1920s and early '30s.

Top left: Enjoy a variety of entrées, including filet mignon. *Bottom left:* The jumbo shrimp cocktail is plated with a sash of lemon and watermelon radish. *Right:* The stunning atrium of the West Baden Hotel features several statues that were part of the 1917 renovation.

Before dining, make a stop in the West Baden Springs Hotel Museum to learn a little more on the history of the property and how it appeared in its heyday. Take a walk on the grounds and explore the sunken garden and remaining springhouse. Watch the horse carriage and train trolley transporting guests around the grounds.

If you're traveling a distance or have a special occasion to celebrate, make a reservation and get the full West Baden experience by staying in one of the 243 luxury guest rooms or suites and paying a visit to the spa for a treatments.

Other dining options on-site include Sinclair's, Cafe Sinclair's and Table One, an exquisite private dining experience for up to 10 that features a customized, five-course menu.

8538 W Baden Ave., West Baden Springs, 844-291-7465
frenchlick.com

WHISTLE STOP
RESTAURANT & MUSEUM

This museum and café will wow railroad fans

If you love the history and romance of trail travel, you might consider paying a visit to Whistle Stop Restaurant & Museum in Monon. Not only can you enjoy a hearty lunch or pile your plate high from the salad bar, but you can step back in time as you make your way through this museum that celebrates railway history with a big focus on Indiana.

The museum stemmed from the personal collection of Dale Ward that began in 1994. As a local quarry owner, Ward's only connection to the railroad was that the rock excavated from his quarry was transported by railcar. Still, his fascination with rail history and his collection (which was housed at his home) quickly grew so large that it needed a bigger space. It later moved to its current home, where additions were made to accommodate the expanding collection. Part of the site now makes up the Monon Connection Train Museum. In another part, you can sit down to a meal while model trains roll by on tracks overhead.

The museum houses the largest private railroad collection in the country that is shared with the public. Among its 6,500-plus pieces are more than 280 railroad lanterns, plus china, silver, whistles, chimes, padlocks, keys, railroad police badges, watches, signs, and more. There's also a large number of bells, four of which are from the Civil War period or earlier.

The centerpiece of the exhibit is its "mansion on wheels," a luxury train car built in 1898 for a cost of $40,000 by one of the founders of the Standard Oil Company, Henry Flagler, for his wife to travel in. It features a stunning chandelier in the dining area, hand-carved white mahogany from the Canary Islands, 30 Tiffany glass windows, four

Left: Classic burgers and sandwiches are a big feature on the menu where you'll find items with cute railroad-themed names. *Center:* The "Train Wreck" is a baked potato loaded with a pile of pulled pork, cheese sauce, sour cream, scallions and jalapeño slices. *Right:* The Whistle Stop Restaurant & Museum has railroad memorabilia on display big and small both indoors and out.

toilets, and one of the first train cars to have a fireplace in it, which was covered in white onyx from Pakistan.

Another room contains a full-sized replica of an Illinois Central depot made from original blueprints filled with artifacts collected from abandoned train depots. The tour also includes a room with a large HO scale train layout. The guided tour runs about an hour, but you'll also want to plan time to examine all the train memorabilia and equipment on the grounds outside, as well.

Now, on to the food. There's a sizable list of classic diner food and more: burgers, wings, sandwiches, steaks, pork chops, salads. Some of the items carry the train theme. The Train Wreck is a loaded baked potato piled high with pulled pork, cheese sauce, sour cream, scallions, and jalapeños. Railroad Ties are deep-fried chicken tenders. If you're feeling extra hungry, try the Cowcatcher, a half-pound burger patty topped with ham; American, Swiss, and Jack cheeses; bacon; onion rings; and barbecue sauce.

The place is family friendly and includes kids' meals on the menu—kids, both small and big, will have a blast here. Discounts are offered for seniors and also military, veterans, and first responders.

10012 US-421, Monon, 219-253-4100
mononconnection.net

HENRY'S

Meet me at Henry's

The front of the menu reads "Meet Me at Henry's." And customers have been doing so since 1959. Henry's restaurant in Fort Wayne opened as a small tavern in a building built in 1875. It featured an ornate Brunswick wood bar that had been moved there in 1942 from the nearby Berry Cafe, which hosted sports, media, and theatrical personalities of the late 1800s and early 1900s.

Today it's a cozy, casual restaurant where you can enjoy consistently good food while you soak up the nostalgia. Henry Freistroffer started the business that 65 years later is being run by his son, John.

Walking in, you can't help but wonder what it would have been like to sit at the bar decades ago or in one of the dark wood booths with a mirror and lined with little lamps. It's one of those places that hasn't changed much over the years, but in a wonderful way. A few vintage decor pieces, like a wooden cigarette machine, hint back to the earlier days of the business.

The menu is constantly evolving, being changed up every six months, but it maintains a variety of sandwiches, burgers, steaks, and seafood. Some of the most popular items are the Reuben sandwich, fried fish, and pork tenderloin. Meats are fresh and sourced locally, and all steaks are grilled to order and leveled up by a burgundy wine-infused steak butter. Soups, salads, and dressings are made from scratch.

Decadent desserts are made locally by Purple Mountain—chocolate cake and cheesecake varieties.

Make your visit to this one a date night for the grown-ups. You must be 21 to enter. Henry's opens daily at 4 p.m. and stays open for the night owls until 3 a.m.

The dining room features an ornate Brunswick wood bar.

536 W Main St., Fort Wayne, 260-426-0531
henrysftwayne.com

The massive wooden bar was produced by Brunswick, a company started by Swiss immigrant and master woodworker John Brunswick in 1845 at age 14. He started out making carriages and opened a sales office in Chicago in 1848. The company went on to produce billiard tables, bowling alleys, school furniture, and more.

ADAMS STREET CHOPHOUSE

19th-century homestead is now swanky steak house

There's a lot of history to the 1852 Greek Revival mansion at 617 Adams Street in Muncie. It was one of the first homesteads in the area and remains one of the area's oldest structures, built for Thomas Neely. Neely was born in 1811 in Pennsylvania and moved to Muncie in 1839. He was an early businessman in the area, first operating a grocery store and later a blacksmith shop and then a photography studio. He also campaigned to bring the first railroad to Muncie.

He was active in the community, serving on the county board as a school director. He was elected to the board of education and played a significant role in the establishment of Muncie's first high school.

In 1860, Neely began keeping a daily diary, which continued until his death in 1901. He chronicled his life on his homestead and progress of his garden on grounds that now house an upscale steak house. The bulk of that diary collection is in the archives at nearby Ball State University.

The home had recently served as a fine-dining restaurant with decor set in the period when the Neely family lived there. When Chad Massoth bought the business, he wanted to keep it as an upscale dining experience, but he fast-forwarded the era a few decades. Different rooms have different themes, but the overall vibe is one that takes you back to the glamour of the roaring '20s through the Rat Pack era of the '40s and '50s. It's full of timeless charm that provides a perfect backdrop for a fine meal.

> Not crazy about vegetables? You will be after you try their glazed carrots, which have a sweet, syrupy sauce that makes you feel like you're eating a slice of french toast.

Left: There are several rooms for guests to enjoy, each of them harkening back to yesteryear. *Right:* A historic home built for an early Muncie businessman, Thomas Neely, serves as the setting for the Adams Street Chophouse.

The downstairs Adams Street Room is adorned with deep green walls, Art Deco influences, and photos of stars of Hollywood's golden era with an adjoining speakeasy. Upstairs are the Frank Sinatra Room and the Rat Pack Room. Pumping through speakers are the sounds of varied artists with a leaning toward entertainers like Frank Sinatra, Jimmy Durante, and Doris Day.

The goal in transforming the mansion to a top-notch steak house was to serve the best of the best. The restaurant opened in December 2023 serving USDA prime steaks and scallops that are flown in. While the surroundings feel luxurious, it's not at all pretentious. It feels casually elegant and friendly and as likely to satisfy a family as it will a lone business professional.

The menu includes something for everyone, from casual burgers to comforting grilled meat loaf to an orange chicken bowl to pan-seared duck breast. However, the place really shines when you look further at the seafood and steak selections. Pescatarians will love the seared diver scallops, chilean sea bass, salmon fillet, and shrimp with gouda grits.

Steaks are USDA prime that have been hand selected by trained professionals at Stock Yard Meats, including a barrel-cut filet that is rare to see on a restaurant menu. You can also get sizable bone-in New York strips, porterhouses, and a 22-ounce cowboy-cut rib eye. Optional accoutrements of béarnaise, baby portobellos, bacon bleu cheese, and more can be ordered to enhance your steak.

617 E Adams St., Muncie, 765-283-4838
adamsstreetchophouse.com

SOUTH SIDE SODA SHOP

Retro diner with a modern twist

If you like a bit of nostalgia with your meal, you'll enjoy dining at South Side Soda Shop. Constructed in the early 1900s, the building where South Side Soda Shop resides was first opened as a grocery store with a soda fountain added in the 1940s, making it a popular neighborhood soda shop. It also served simultaneously as a post office and bus stop.

New owners took over in 1986, and soon their daughter and son-in-law Nick and Charity Boyd bought the business. It's truly a family endeavor, with the Boyds' two daughters involved in the business and a fourth generation who is getting their feet wet helping out after school.

A dining car was added on in 1994 to accommodate more customers and add to the vintage vibe and 1950s feel. Inside are cozy booths and steel tables with vinyl padded chairs. The red, black, and white color scheme is a throwback with vintage sports flags, a jukebox, a peanut machine, old Coca-Cola signs, and other hints of yesteryear.

Nick Boyd grew up in Philadelphia and Charity is from Detroit. Several items on the menu come from family recipes or ones that Nick missed from his childhood, like the turtle soup, the liverwurst and bacon sandwich, and the Philly cheesesteak, which is their most popular menu item. Hoagie rolls for the sandwiches come directly from Amoroso's Bakery in Philadelphia. They also have a Swedish-style limpa bread, which is a light rye with orange zest.

As you'd expect at an old-fashioned soda shop, you can get yourself a classic burger and fries, but also so much more. You'll be surprised at what's offered on the menu. Lump meat crab cakes. Oysters on the half shell. Lake Superior whitefish. Shrimp cocktail.

Left: A '50s-style diner just isn't complete without a vintage jukebox. *Center:* Sipping on a milkshake or malt seems appropriate in this fun vintage atmosphere. *Right:* A vintage dining car was added on to the building in 1994.

In addition to hoagies and seafood specials are such entrées as soda shop spaghetti and meatballs, chicken salad, fried clams, hot dogs, and grilled pork tenderloins. They serve an award-winning chili that was voted "Best in Michiana." They also have a Philly Chili, similar to something Nick enjoyed on Christmas Eve growing up. It's chili served over noodles, topped with onions, freshly shredded cheese, and sour cream that is served in a soda glass. It was one of the foods featured when Guy Fieri came to visit during the first season of *Diners, Drive-Ins and Dives.*

There's also a special item served on Wednesdays: a sloppy joe recipe from the original owners that was the first hot food served in the building.

The original soda fountain is still in use, and an ice cream case is full of tasty flavors. You can get a number of sweet treats, from sundaes to banana splits to malts to floats. Also, don't leave without trying some pie. There are 33 flavors of home-baked pies, along with another dozen and a half cakes and cheesecakes.

1122 S Main St., Goshen, 574-534-3790
southsidesodashop.com

UNION HALL RESTAURANT AT JOURNEYMAN DISTILLERY'S AMERICAN FACTORY

Former factory building becomes multiuse campus with elevated American fare

Building upon their recipe for success with Journeyman Distillery in Three Oaks, Michigan, Bill and Johanna Welter set upon a similar, yet grander journey by opening a second location in Bill's hometown of Valparaiso in 2023 and reviving another abandoned factory with a new purpose.

In 2010, they cofounded Journeyman Distillery and placed it in the Historic Register building that was once home to the former Warren Featherbone Company in Three Oaks, which dates back to 1883. The distillery houses a restaurant, private and retail spaces and an 18-hole putting green inspired by a Scottish putting course.

The location was originally one of the first woolen mills in Porter County, established just after the Civil War. It later served as a wagon and carriage company, soap company, pin factory and most recently the Anco windshield wiper factory. It saw little use after Anco closed in the 1960s.

After years of planning and renovation, the American Factory opened to the public in the fall of 2023. Transformed were 140,000 square feet of the former factory site, divided into sections to create a

Left: The cocktail menu has a creative mix of drinks made with quality Journeyman spirits. *Center:* An existing water tower on the old factory site has been repainted with the Journeyman name. *Right:* Following a tour of the campus, guests can enjoy a tasting in the retail space of premium spirits.

destination campus including multiple restaurants, a brewery, a rooftop bar, a karaoke bar, private event spaces, a retail store, and an outdoor whiskey garden with performance stage.

In designing the spaces, glimpses of the past have been preserved in signage, lighting, and other features that give a nod to its industrial history.

Besides spirits, the retail store carries everything from cocktail accessories to apparel to their house-made barbecue sauce, ketchup, barrel-aged maple syrup, and much more.

In the store, you'll find their most popular spirits and special limited-run varieties, like the Popcorn Bourbon Whiskey produced in honor of Orville Redenbacher, whose popcorn company was once located in Valparaiso, and the annual Popcorn Fest that the city holds each fall.

In Union Hall, you can choose from a creative menu of signature cocktails along with barrel-aged classics and elevated, out-of-the-box starters and entrees, with several vegetarian, vegan and gluten-free options.

Best-selling sandwiches are the smashburger, grilled cheese and the btb turkey schnitzel. The menu highlights ingredients using spirits, including Lincoln Highway Vodka Romesco Sauce, Fine Girl Brandy Gravy, and Black Hearts Gin creamed spinach.

258 S Campbell St., Valparaiso, 219-510-1300
journeyman.com/unionhall

NICK'S KITCHEN

Originator of the breaded pork tenderloin

If there's one sandwich that is synonymous with the Hoosier State, it's the breaded pork tenderloin. This crunchy, oversized piece of pounded pork is hand breaded and deep-fried to golden perfection. Then it is plated on a bun that is dwarfed by its size.

You'll find them on menus all over the state, from diners to breweries to food trucks to family restaurants to festivals and more. And each one is a little different than the next thanks to modified cooking methods, special ingredients, or secrets that will never be spilled.

In Huntington, you'll find a little diner that is said to be the first to serve up a BPT with a recipe dating back to 1904. Nick Freienstein had been running a pushcart and then a sandwich stand outside of the Huntington County Courthouse for a few years before he was able to open his own brick-and-mortar eatery. It was a modest, narrow, empty lot between two buildings.

He convinced the owners next door to let him use their existing walls and construct a front, back, and roof. They agreed and he was in business. In 1908, he opened his doors and began serving up the BPT. It was a variation on the wiener schnitzel that his German immigrant parents introduced him to.

While the business isn't still in Freienstein's family, it has been run by another family for three generations. It was sold three times before Gene and Peggy Drabenstot purchased it in 1969.

Twenty years later, one of their daughters bought the business. Two of her siblings also own restaurants honoring Nick: Nick's Junction in Roanoke and Nick's Country Cafe in Huntington. Nick's Kitchen made national news when Vice President Dan Quayle visited the diner where he had been a frequent visitor when practicing law in Huntington.

Left: Mason Drabenstot, whose grandparents purchased the restaurant in 1969, is shown in front of a mural on the restaurant's back wall. *Top center:* Handmade milkshakes are a frosty treat you won't want to skip. *Bottom center:* The breaded pork tenderloin is so large that it fills most of the plate. *Right:* Nick's Kitchen is said to be the place where the popular Hoosier tenderloin sandwich was invented.

Obviously, the breaded pork tenderloin is the first thing you should try. It's juicy and crunchy and hangs way over the bun. You can also purchase fully cooked frozen tenderloins to take home and reheat. They also ship it out across the country via Gold Belly. Recently they sent 175 to the USS *Indiana* Navy ship along with 20 sugar cream pies.

The official Indiana State Pie, sugar cream pie, is one of their bestsellers. They usually have at least a dozen pie varieties available each day, all made by Mason Drabenstot, a third generation of the family to be involved in the business.

You can order breakfast all day, and it's a great way to enjoy a tenderloin—atop a biscuit and covered in sausage gravy and eggs. Everything is very fresh and high quality. The center tenderloin is used for their BPT, and they grind the trimmings to make their own sausage. Burgers are fresh, hand-formed, and pure ground beef paradise.

506 N Jefferson St., Huntington, 260-356-6618
nicksdowntown.com

Can't decide on a pie flavor? Order a pie flight and get three half slices.

MONTEGO BAY GRILLE

Escape to the tropics in downtown Hobart

If you've ever had one of those days where you just want to skip town and head to a tropical place to sip a fruity cocktail and nosh on seafood, you'll be surprised to know you can get it in Indiana. No need to hop on a plane. Just head to Hobart.

In 2017, the Jamaican restaurant opened on Main Street, bringing a bit of the Caribbean to Northwest Indiana. The dining room seats about 40; additional patio seating gives a picturesque view of Lake George. Sit back and take in a sunset while sipping on cocktails in this lakeside setting.

The eatery specializes in Caribbean fusion that is full of fresh, locally sourced ingredients with seafood as a main character in this island-inspired lineup. Start with the island shrimp tacos, made with their signature jerk sauce and served on warm tortillas with citrus slaw, or the crab cake (one of their signature dishes) of lump crab meat, spicy avocado sauce, marinated heirloom tomatoes, and lime.

Although it may seem more like a dessert, there's a heavenly appetizer of fried plantains that are caramelized with a decadent drizzle. Jerk wings are another starter choice; they're marinated, smoked, grilled, and slathered in jerk sauce.

The signature dishes that they're best known for are the jerk-style chicken, salmon, and pork that are best enjoyed with a side of the red beans and rice.

Chef Teddian is the visionary behind the creative dishes you'll find on the menu. With a robust background in the hotel, cruise, and casino industries, he brings his experience and passion to this fun concept. He has a love of the art of gastronomy, and his commitment

Clockwise, from left: A nice selection of tropical drinks will make you feel like you're on an island with your toes in the sand. The dining room is bright and features eclectic art pieces on the walls. You'll find some nice seafood selections on the menu, like the scallops pictured here. With a nice laid back island vibe to the place, the large portrait of Bob Marley is quite appropriate. Shrimp tacos and plantains give a taste of a more tropical place.

to his craft is evident in every dish. His charming and welcoming personality make the experience that much more wonderful as he adds his personal touch to everything he does.

The colorful, beachy dining room has some nice artwork, including a piece of the GOAT of reggae music, Bob Marley. The music is groovy. The drinks are cold. The vibes are chill.

It's also a great place to groove! Each Thursday you can watch local musicians and bands, listen to acoustic open-mic sessions, or witness talented songwriters bring their melodies, ballads, and rock tunes.

322 Main St., Hobart, 219-940-3152
montegobaygrille.com

THE OVERLOOK RESTAURANT

Get a side of stunning scenery with your meal

You won't find any other restaurant in Indiana that has a view quite as spectacular at The Overlook in the small town of Leavenworth, which has a population of about 300. Situated on the Ohio River, the dining room sits on a bluff with walls of windows where you can see for about 20 miles up and down the Ox Bow Bend of the river.

The restaurant dates back to the late 1930s after a flood wiped out the whole town of Old Leavenworth. Businesses moved up on the bluff to rebuild. A cafe and grocery store opened on the floor above a chicken hatchery that also had gas pumps outside and became a Greyhound bus stop. It eventually got to be called The Overlook and today it welcomes tourists and locals for some hearty home cooking with a stunning view.

Over the years it has gone from a little 32-seat spot to a 123-seat dining room with additional outdoor seating. From homemade soups to fried chicken, there's plenty of comfort food to fill you up. Other house specialities include a Beef Manhattan, Mom's Meatloaf and a Fried Cod Platter. There's also a nice selection of sandwiches, from the reuben to the pork tenderloin to the BBQ bacon cheeseburger and you'll find a number of daily and seasonal specialties rotated through menu. There are also plenty of offering for younger visitors with a kids' menu of favorites, like macaroni and cheese, grilled cheese, chicken tenders and more.

The Spirit of Indiana Wine Tasting room opened in the summer of 2024 in the level beneath the restaurant offering a tranquil space where you can sip as you look out on the water to see wooded riverside hills,

Top: No matter where you sit in the dining room, you'll have a nice view out a wall of windows. *Bottom left:* Located on a bluff in Southern Indiana, you have a view of the Ohio River and Kentucky from the dining room and grounds. *Bottom center:* Meat loaf is one of the comfort food meals you will find on the menu. *Bottom right:* The signature item at The Overlook is their fried chicken, which has a nice crunchy coating.

barges moving down the river and wildlife who call the area home. There's nothing like viewing a gorgeous sunset from this vantage point. The tasting room features wines from Indiana producers, specialty cocktails, Indiana beers, custom pizzas, specialty cakes and charcuterie boards. Paint & Sip classes and wine education opportunities are also planned for the new space.

1153 W SR-62, Leavenworth, 812-739-4264
theoverlook.com

1875: THE STEAKHOUSE AT FRENCH LICK RESORT

Eat and stay where the rich and famous flocked for spring water

In the small towns of French Lick and West Baden are two hotels that represent the opulence of the late 19th century, when the rich and famous traveled by rail seeking the medical benefits of their sulfur springs. They became famous spa towns for athletes, musicians, entertainers, and even gangsters.

The French Lick Springs Hotel boasted its miracle waters and drew guests from miles around. It also became a haven for golfers with its two championship courses. During World War II, it served as a spring training site for both the Chicago Cubs and Chicago White Sox.

The West Baden Hotel was designed to be grander and had an opera house, golf courses, a church, a ball field, and a double-decker pony and bicycle track. After a fire, it was rebuilt in the early 1900s to model grand spas in Europe and became the world's largest free-span dome, dubbed the "Eighth Wonder of the World."

Within the two hotels are several eateries that allow you to dine on amazing food in beautiful, historic spaces.

1875: The Steakhouse is located in the French Lick Springs Hotel, named to commemorate May 17, 1875, the date of the very first Kentucky Derby. The hotel's signature restaurant sits just off the main

> **Another option for romantic fine dining is Sinclair's Restaurant located in the West Baden Springs Hotel.**

Left to right: When at a steakhouse, you have to try the filet. This one is served with a scallop and creamed spinach and roasted garlic mashed potatoes as sides. The steakhouse sits off the elegant lobby of the French Lick Hotel. Along with your bread basket, you are brought an appetizer of tomato juice. The beverage was invented at the French Lick Hotel when a chef ran out of oranges, but had an abundance of tomatoes. There are a number of elevated appetizer options to choose from, including the jumbo crab cake over black bean salsa.

lobby offering an elegant atmosphere and open kitchen. It overlooks the stunning gardens and iconic Pluto Springs gazebo.

On the menu are cuts of beef that are 100 percent premium-aged Midwest, corn-fed Angus. Start with Wagyu meatballs with herbed ricotta, baked lobster mac and cheese, or a jumbo crab cake. Or put your spoon in a bowl of their luxurious lobster bisque or zesty potato and chorizo soup.

For any steak connoisseur, this is paradise. From the petite 8-ounce filet mignon or baseball-cut sirloin to the 14-ounce New York Strip to the 24-ounce cowboy-cut rib eye, there's something for the smallest or biggest of appetites and lots of accompaniments to dress it up—blue cheese sauce or blackberry glaze or béarnaise or hollandaise. Or go all out and enjoy it Oscar style. Add mushrooms, horseradish butter, diver scallops or sautéed onions for a luxe finish.

The wine list is extensive, and the menu has perfect pairings indicated with each item.

8670 W SR-56, French Lick, 866-321-5884
frenchlick.com

TYLER'S TENDER

Have your meal delivered to you via model train

If you've got little ones to entertain and want to stay as far away as possible from the madness of Chuck E. Cheese or a similar family entertainment spot, Tyler's Tender is a good place to consider, especially if you or those little ones are fans of trains.

Established in 2007, it was the creation of parents of young kids who wanted an alternative for moms and dads when dining out with their kids. At the time their young boys were fans of Thomas the Tank Engine. It became a place that was just as enticing to older generations who loved the nostalgic feelings that come with everything choo-choo trains.

The train theme is carried throughout the full-service restaurant with an O-scale model train on display, a private room with model trains running on a track overhead, and a kid-sized train that kids can ride on.

As if that were not enough, you can sit at a stool at the counter and have your order delivered to you on a model flatbed train car. It doesn't get any cooler than that. It's a great space to hold a birthday party, and they also have a birthday club you can sign up for where children will get a free treat during their birthday month.

And if you or the kids are still longing for a little bit of the entertainment center experience, the adjoining storefront is a small arcade where you can rack up points playing games to trade in for little prize trinkets.

> Stop in during their 2 to 5 p.m. "Happy Hour" for special deals like $1 milkshakes, free train rides, or half off on appetizers.

Left: A large u-shaped counter with stools has a train track that runs around it to deliver food in a basket by miniature train car. *Top right:* An arcade room serves as entertainment while kids wait for food to be prepared. *Bottom right:* The train makes its way out of the kitchen to deliver meals to customers at the counter.

For being a place that is so appealing to kids, they definitely cater to adult appetites on the food menu, too. They've got the mandatory kid favorites like chicken nuggets, hot dogs, mac and cheese, pizza, and grilled cheese and also adult-appropriate grub like a pot roast melt, fish and chips, wraps, and a strawberry spinach salad.

A nice bonus of this place is that side options aren't just french fries and chips. You can also get fresh broccoli, coleslaw, fresh fruit, or a side salad. Additionally, with each kid meal, you can also opt for mashed potatoes, a fruit cup, applesauce, apple slices, or mandarin oranges.

350 E US-30, Schererville, 219-322-5590
tylerstender.com

145

STORY INN

One inconvenient location since 1851

Located in Brown County, Story is a charming, one-of-a-kind town. It dates back to 1851 and is isolated with one road leading into town that dead-ends on the other side. There's a total population of three, as nearly all the buildings in the small community are part of the Story Inn.

It is named for Dr. George Story, who received a land grant for the property from President Millard Fillmore. He built the early buildings in what was the largest settlement in the area at the time. At one time it had two general stores, a church, a one-room schoolhouse, a grain mill, a sawmill, a slaughterhouse, a blacksmith shop, and a post office.

The Great Depression brought an end to Story's days of prosperity as families left their farms in search of work. With so much land abandoned, the State of Indiana purchased 16,000 acres of wooded hills that became Brown County State Park. Additional acres were acquired later that became Hoosier National Forest and Yellowwood State Forest. In 1960, the US Army Corps of Engineers flooded nearby land to create Lake Monroe, which cut off direct access to Bloomington. Public land now surrounds Story on three sides.

Once a general store that was rebuilt after a fire in 1916, the Story Inn is now a destination farm-to-table restaurant with lodging. The property is a National Historic District, something that was accomplished by Rick Hofstetter, who had purchased the 17-acre town at a sheriff's sale in 1998. Since his passing in 2019, Story is now in the hands of Hofstetter's son, Rich.

Fifteen buildings in the district are deemed to be contributing to that historic character with the Wheeler-Hedrick General Store being the town's centerpiece. There's also an old grain mill, barns, and outbuildings.

Left: As you enter the small town of Story, you're greeted by vintage signs. *Right:* Upscale entrées are created with fresh, local ingredients.

The Story Inn has four available rooms, and there are 11 cabins that can be rented. It has become a popular destination for weddings and weekend getaways.

There is now an 1851 Club, which has individual, family, and company sponsorship plans and availability for guests to book the whole town.

As for the dining portion of Story, the dining room within the Story Inn offers a prix fixe menu. The menu changes each week with Chef Doug Talley utilizing food grown on-site and sourced from local providers. Each dinner is five to seven courses, including prepicked appetizers and dessert. Diners are able to choose from among main course options. The leisurely two-hour candlelight dining experience in this historic structure is like no other and well worth venturing off the beaten path for.

The restaurant is also open for weekend brunch with a number of classic entrées that include sides of sausage, bacon, and home fries, along with brunch-time beverages. The lower-level tavern offers a lineup of casual sandwiches.

6404 IN-135, Nashville, 812-988-2273
storyinn.com

THE SUPER BURGER

Ag teacher brings farm-to-fork concept to classroom

The small town of Paoli (population 3,600) is probably best known for the Paoli Peaks Ski Resort, which produces artificial snow to keep the winter attraction going year after year. But it's also a place where you'll get one of the best burgers in Indiana.

The Super Burger has been an institution in Paoli for decades. Teachers Coy and Maya Scott bought the iconic eatery in 2013. As an agriculture teacher at the local high school, Coy incorporated the restaurant into the curriculum. Through fundraising done by his students, it started out with a single pig and has grown to a full-scale working barn maintained by students. The program supplies many of the pork products served at the restaurant.

Throughout the restaurant are photos and jerseys honoring past and present local athletes, which helps create a sense of community when you come in to enjoy a burger or pork tenderloin. Naturally, it's a fun hangout for teens who know the owners from school, and many high schoolers have worked jobs there making food and serving customers.

The food is fresh and cooked to order and has a big variety with something for everyone. Sandwiches make up the bulk of the orders, with everything from a traditional Super Cheeseburger to a pizza burger to a fish sandwich to a sloppy joe. One unique feature on the menu is that you can order your burger with ground beef or ground turkey for a leaner serving.

> **The Super Burger is part of the Indiana Foodway's Burger Trail.**

Top: High School sports memorabilia lines the walls. *Bottom, left to right:* Patio seating is available outside The Super Burger. The Triple Newk is a triple cheeseburger with bacon that has been named one of the best in the state. A customer enjoys The Moby, an 8-ounce cod fillet.

There are some quirky signature items that customers like to take on, though few succeed in finishing. One is The Triple Newk (named after the high school athletic director). It has three quarter-pound patties, three layers of cheese, and three layers of bacon and is served on a bed of cheese fries. The Ram is a jumbo tenderloin topped with barbecue pork, bacon, and slaw. The Moby is a giant 8-ounce cod fillet with slaw, fries, and hush puppies.

There are over two dozen different sides to choose from, including waffle fries, fried pickles, sweet corn nuggets, and cottage cheese. Creamy shakes and malts can be made from any of their 30 different flavors.

600 W Main St., Paoli, 812-723-4445

SANTA'S CANDY CASTLE

Sweet treats taste even sweeter in this castle in a charming Christmas town

Did you know that Indiana has a town named Santa Claus? It's a place where much of the commerce is connected to the Christmas holiday or the big guy in red whom you may also know as Kris Kringle, Father Christmas, Saint Nick, or other monikers.

The town named in his honor was founded in 1854 and was originally called Santa Fe. When town leaders were unable to establish a post office because there was already a Santa Fe, Indiana, they mulled over new names and held town meetings. The town was renamed in 1856.

With a name like Santa Claus, it is only fitting that Christmas seems to extend all year long here. Several statues of Mr. Claus can be found around town. Businesses carry themes of Christmas and the North Pole. The big amusement park in town that draws tens of thousands of visitors each year opened as Santa Claus Land in 1946 and later changed to Holiday World. Beside it is the Sun Outdoors Lake Rudolph Camp Resort. A Santa Claus museum and village is a popular stop for visitors, as is the Santa Claus Store, which sells Christmas decor and gifts year-round. Kringle Place is a holiday-themed shopping center selling all things Christmas. A local mini-golf spot is called Frosty's Fun Center. Santa's Lodge is a rustic, Christmas-themed lodge.

There's also a castle in Santa Claus—a candy castle, that is. The historic brick castle was dedicated in 1935 and was the first building in Santa Claus Town, the nation's first themed attraction. The castle originally was sponsored by the Curtiss Candy Company of Chicago, creators of the Baby Ruth and Butterfinger candy bars.

The building was designed by artist Emil Strauss to give a look of existing in a fairy tale land. It is made of red brick with a tower, turret,

Left: Santa's Candy Castle was dedicated in 1935. *Center:* The castle was originally sponsored by the Curtiss Candy Company of Chicago, who created Baby Ruth and Butterfinger candy bars. *Right:* The frozen hot chocolate is a perfect treat after a long day at the Holiday World Theme Park & Splashin' Safari Water Park.

and rotunda. Santa Claus Town once had a Toy Village that consisted of over half a dozen miniature fairy tale buildings, each sponsored by a prominent national toy manufacturer, and had a woodshop where Santa Claus could be seen making wooden toys by hand. The castle that was once filled with toys is now filled with candy.

Many years later, after Santa Claus Land ceased operations, the castle was restored, and it opened in 2006 as Santa's Candy Castle, a store that specializes in all things sugary and sweet. You'll find rooms and shelves of just about any candy you can imagine. There are plenty of nostalgic candy items and homemade fudge.

There's a vibe that takes you back to childhood and turns you into a kid again. Find all your favorite throwback candies in this unique castle.

15499 N SR-245, Santa Claus, 800-356-1935

> **Don't leave without trying a frozen hot chocolate, a refreshing frozen treat that tastes especially good after a busy summer day on the rides at Holiday World.**

MOSER'S AUSTRIAN CAFE

Authentic flavors of Austria in Northern Indiana

Werner Moser grew up learning to cook with his parents in his home kitchen in Austria. It seemed like it was what he was meant to do. He came to the US in 1982, and in 1999, he finally achieved his dream of having a kitchen of his own where he could introduce those specialties to people in Indiana.

The decor is reminiscent of his homeland with photos and memorabilia of the region donning the walls of this vintage building, authentic dress worn by employees, and occasional live music of bands with tubas and fancy alpine horns.

In 2021, Moser hung up his apron for retirement, but the restaurant, revelry, and recipes live on. New owners are Derrick and Margaret Czarnecki, who owned the business next door called Carlisle Coffee and Sweets. The bakery makes a variety of desserts, including the signature apple strudel served at Moser's.

Not much changed when they took over. Moser had a good thing going, and if it ain't broke, why try and fix it? They did bring back longtime cook Brad Breneman as head chef, who had previously spent over a decade working in the kitchen at Moser's. So, the schnitzel goes on.

Speaking of schnitzel, the restaurant offers more than 14 variations of wiener schnitzel—the pounded and breaded veal entrée. You can get it in its purest form with just a squeeze of lemon or you can get a variety of toppings, from wine, cheese, or barbecue sauces to mushrooms and onions to various cheeses. Whichever one you choose, it will come with a scoop of traditional spaetzle and shredded red cabbage, just like in Moser's home country. It will also come with hearty breads and spreads and your choice of soup or salad. Austrian-inspired soups include liver dumpling soup and cheese dumpling soup.

Left: The dining room is filled with Austrian and German decor and memorabilia, including a beer stein collection. Center: The interior has exposed brick walls and different European accents throughout. Right: Located in a historic building, Moser's Austrian Cafe has indoor and outdoor dining.

Other dinner entrées include schweinsbrater, a slow-cooked pork roast with caraway seed and garlic; schlemmerpfandl, a combo of house steak, pork medallions, and chicken breast with a bacon cream sauce; or the sausage platter, where you can choose between bratwurst, debreziner, theuringer, or weisswurst served with sauerkraut, potatoes, and German mustard.

Among the appetizers are a grilled portobello mushroom, a Bavarian meat and cheese platter, potato pancakes, and a giant soft pretzel with German mustard and house-made olive spread.

And don't forget the beer! You'll find many European brews to choose from to accompany your taste of Austria—labels like Paulaner and Hacker Pschorr.

201-203 E Michigan St., New Carlisle, 574-654-0086
moserscarlisle.com

BLUE TOP DRIVE-IN

Put on your poodle skirt and cruise on over to this nostalgic classic car magnet

Sometimes, don't you wish you could go back to a different time when jukeboxes rather than cell phones provided entertainment? Blue Top Drive-In is that place. One of the oldest establishments in Highland, the Blue Top has been a gathering spot for automobile enthusiasts for decades. Originally located across the street from its current location on Indianapolis Boulevard, it opened in 1939. In 1964, the current location was built, and it's a place where time seems to stand still—in the best possible way.

While many such places tend to be seasonal dining spots, this one is open year-round. However, it's in summer when it really gets rockin' and rollin'.

On busy summer nights, it's like being right back in the 1960s with muscle cars galore parked side by side, their windows rolled down partially to accommodate the tray loaded with freshly made burgers and creamy milkshakes while music of the era plays.

The car enthusiasts who make their way to the drive-in are a huge part of the charm. It's like a car cruise or a classic car show on any given day when you'll see cars of all eras pulling in or parked with the hood up so that onlookers can get a good view.

You can opt to dine in your car or park and eat at picnic tables, which is what a lot of classic car owners will do rather than risk spilling ketchup on the interior of their baby. Carhops in poodle skirts take and deliver your orders to you.

Inside is a whole other nostalgic throwback with barstools, vintage signs, old records, and other 1950s and '60s photos and memorabilia lining the walls. You feel like you're in an episode of *Happy Days*, and you can't help but be happy when you're there.

Left: Picnic tables are lined outside for more dining space. *Center:* While many customers pull up and order from their cars, there's also a dining room if you'd rather eat at a table. *Top right:* Burgers are a staple on the Blue Top menu. *Bottom right:* The Blue Top Drive-In in Highland has not changed much on the outside since its opening.

The signature Big Ben burger, a fully dressed double cheeseburger, is named for the original owner. The drive-in was formerly called Johnsen's Blue Top Drive-In, but now it's John's Blue Top Drive-In. Current owner John Golfis is a big car guy and loves the history of the '50s and '60s drive-in heyday era, and he's done his best to preserve it for generations to come.

Along with keeping classics on the menu, like the Big Ben, he has expanded the menu offerings, adding things like gyros, oven-roasted chicken, wraps, stuffed peppers, and chicken sandwiches on gourmet buns.

He's also proud of the milkshake selections. There are around 50 different shakes to choose from, many of them utilizing various breakfast cereals.

8801 Indianapolis Blvd., Highland, 219-838-1233

Keep an eye on their calendar for special events, from Elvis impersonators to movie nights to Easter bunny visits.

NICK'S ENGLISH HUT

"Sink the Biz" at this College Bar and Restaurant

Once you're in the doors of Nick's English Hut in Bloomington, you can't take a step in any direction without being inundated with hints that you are in Hoosier Country. This iconic college bar near the Indiana University campus has been around for nearly a century, opening in 1927 as a 50-seat candy store and sandwich shop. In 1934, they received a liquor license, and the business expanded over the years to add a backroom on the lower level and three rooms upstairs. Today, it has seating for over 500.

Nick Hrisomalos made his way to the U.S. from Greece at age 14 aboard a ship. Having just an eighth-grade education, he went to work in the Illinois steel mills before returning to serve in the Greek Army during the first Balkan War. He was drafted into the US Army in 1918, but his service was cut short by a case of the Spanish Flu, and he was discharged. He then settled in Bloomington, running several different businesses before opening Nick's in 1927.

Business was especially good following World War II when 8 million veterans went to school through the GI Bill and sales more than doubled, and also when Indiana University won the NCAA Championships in 1941, 1953, 1976, 1981 and 1987.

The expansion of the business has included adding "The Attic" room upstairs in 1967, the "Hump Room" in 1979, and the "Hoosier Room" in 2000. Upstairs the walls are lined with jerseys, photos, and other memorabilia of Hoosier players.

The owners support local farmers and use quality ingredients. For their burgers, they use Black Angus Premium natural beef, hormone-free and antibiotic-free beef from a century-plus-old farm near Jasper.

Pizza is made from the original 1953 recipe of Dick Barnes, a former owner of Nick's English Pub who brought Italian-style pizza

Top left: Nick's English Hut is a favorite among college students, locals, and tourists. *Bottom left:* The long first-floor dining room of this college bar island with booths next to walls covered in photos of University of Bloomington sports teams. *Center:* An eclectic mix of decor covers the wall, from license plates to stuffed deer heads to University of Indiana memorabilia. *Right:* The Sink the Biz Fries are a signature appetizer of fries tossed in Romano cheese and Nick's spice blend with garlic mayonnaise for dipping. It's named for a popular drinking game at the bar.

to Bloomington and owned several other restaurants. Other specialties include the Italian Beef and the Stromboli sandwich of crumbled Italian sausage, mozzarella, onion, and Nick's pizza sauce on a baked sub bun.

While Nick's has entertained countless college students over the years, it's also come to be a family eatery in the afternoons and early evenings on the restaurant side. When the rowdy college crowd is there, they play a game that is unique to Nick's called "Sink the Biz." A metal bucket is filled with beer, and a beer glass (the biz) is placed inside. Players take turns pouring beer from their glass into the biz until it sinks. Whoever is responsible for sinking the glass has to drink it.

423 E Kirkwood Ave., Bloomington, 812-332-4040
nicksenglishhut.com

> A fun appetizer is the Sink the Biz fries, a bucket of fries tossed in Romano cheese and Nick's spices with garlic mayonnaise for dipping.

JOSEPH DECUIS

Upscale American dining with beef sourced from family's own Wagyu farm

How far are you willing to drive for a fabulous meal? The correct answer is: as long as it takes to get to Joseph Decuis. Really. It's that amazing of an experience.

The AAA Four Diamond fine-dining farm-to-fork restaurant is worthy of all the accolades it has been bestowed and lives up to all the hype. But the appeal goes beyond it being a beautiful atmosphere with wonderful food. They serve up Wagyu beef, which they raise on their own farm situated just six miles down the road. It's been hailed as some of the finest Wagyu outside of Japan. As far as they know, it's the only Wagyu farm in the country raising beef exclusively for their restaurant guests and market customers. They also grow an abundance of produce in the field and hoop house, have a hops garden, and raise chickens and hogs.

The restaurant is a series of rooms and spaces, each very different from the next. An original bank vault now serves as a wine cellar.

The Exhibition dining room includes the Chairman's Table for up to eight guests, and the Chef's Counter, available by special reservation, where you eat overlooking the open kitchen and enjoy a multicourse chef's choice menu. There's a display showing you which cuts are being showcased at that time. There's a framed letter documenting the prestigious genetics of their cattle. In addition to the AAA Four Diamond Award, they've been grand champion Triple Crown Wagyu

> **Make your dinner part of an extended getaway with an overnight at their inn or bed-and-breakfast on the farm.**

Top left: Dining at Joseph Decuis is a luxurious experience. *Bottom left:* The kitchen staff pauses for a photograph. *Right:* Salads are lined up for serving, made with ingredients grown on the nearby farm operated by the restaurant.

Award winners and earned Best of Award of Excellence from *Wine Spectator.* It's become one of the state's most highly awarded restaurants.

Next door to the restaurant is the Joseph Decuis Emporium, a café and market where you can purchase some of their farm-fresh ingredients. While all of the prime cuts of beef are used exclusively in the restaurant, the shop stocks some of the other cuts that are not in as high demand, like chuck roast, burgers, and flank steak.

Owners Pete and Alice Eshelman met in New York, where Pete was working for the New York Yankees and Alice was an actress. A former baseball player whose career was cut short by injury, Pete went into the sports and entertainment insurance business and eventually opened an office in Indiana. Since the couple was entertaining clients at their farm, they decided to purchase an old bank building to turn into private dining for the company. Four years later, in 2000, they opened it to the public; since then they've expanded, acquiring additional adjoining buildings.

So who was Joseph Decuis (pronounced Do-queeze)? He was a French ancestor of owner Pete Eshelman who lived in New Orleans in the 1800s. His grandfather immigrated in 1720, and the family's story is an inspiring one of living the American dream.

191 N Main St., Roanoke, 260-672-1715
josephdecuis.com

CHICORY CAFÉ

Enjoy a taste of N'Awlins in South Bend

When you're craving a good cup of coffee and something sweet, you've got lots of options, from the fast-food drive-through to cozy mom-and-pop places. But unless you're in Louisiana, where are you going to go for a cup of coffee and some sweets and be immersed in the vibe and flavors of NOLA? Turns out you only need to go to South Bend. And if you're looking for something beyond a cup of joe and beignets, they've got that, too.

The vibe of this place is chill and laid back, just like the Big Easy. Eclectic decor and hues of purple take you to a place far from the worries and hustle of your normal day. The menu is full of tastes of N'Awlins cuisine and a quiet spot during the day, but at night it's all Mardi Gras with live music, karaoke, food and drink specials, trivia, and more.

If breakfast is your jam, you can get it all day long. Biscuits and gravy made with a blend of regular pork sausage and chorizo. House-made Belgian waffles made fresh to order. Egg-filled po'boy sandwiches. Quiche. Avocado toast. It may be hard to make your pick. Soup, sandwiches, flatbreads, and small plates are also offered later in the day.

There are some more standard menu items, like a Cobb salad, Triple Grilled Cheese, or chef salad, but also a good variety of regional dishes or ones that have a New Orleans twist. Of course, you won't want to miss the jambalaya, seafood gumbo, Cajun po'boys, muffuletta, or beignets. Along with your food, select from a number of coffees, teas, lattes, and other tasty beverages—or for something a little stronger, their signature Hurricane or a Big Easy Bloody Mary.

Left: A mural of jazz musicians is displayed on the patio area of the Mishawaka location. *Center:* The Chicory Café locations in South Bend and Mishawaka have a New Orleans theme. *Right:* Delicate, airy, sweet beignets are a must try.

Bring the little ones because there are some nice meal selections that kids are sure to like, including mac and cheese and a waffle with bacon or sausage.

Mark your calendar to be there for Mardi Gras, where you'll find one of the best parties of its kind outside of Louisiana. Its location in the heart of downtown makes it convenient and fun in the center of activity.

The original location opened in 2005, and in 2019, they added a location in Mishawaka near the St. Joseph River with a cute outdoor patio area. It's the perfect place to sit back, relax, and enjoy some great flavors.

It was named a Tripadvisor Travelers' Choice in 2020.

105 E Jefferson Blvd., Ste. 103, South Bend, 574-234-1141
chicorycafe.net

THE NASHVILLE HOUSE

Serving up old-fashioned hospitality one fried biscuit with apple butter at a time

Brown County is a picturesque place where tourists flock for the rolling hills, natural beauty, wineries, eateries, and small-town charm. It is especially stunning in the fall season when the changing leaves create the most stunning of tapestries. It also is an inspiring area for artists of all kinds and is known for the Brown County Art Colony, which formed in 1907 and resulted in the creation of an art guild and gallery that still operates in downtown Nashville.

Nashville is the county seat and is the kind of place that Hallmark movies are made of. An adorable main street. Friendly shop owners. Small businesses. A slower pace. Fascinating history. The town of Nashville is actually the only incorporated town in the county with a total population of about 15,000. It has the highest concentration of forested land of any of Indiana's 92 counties.

One of the most prominent buildings in Nashville's quaint downtown is The Nashville House. The wood building was Brown County's first hotel, built in 1859. It hosted locals, travelers, loggers, and artists, and it's still a respite for hungry souls.

In 1927, A.J. Rogers and Fred Bates Johnson purchased the property and did some remodeling. It was officially christened The Nashville House. In 1943, a fire unfortunately burned it to the ground, but it was quickly rebuilt by Jack Rogers. This new building didn't have guest rooms but became a draw for the famous home cooking and old-time general store.

Jack's son, Andy, took over the business in 1959, adding some slight modern touches but keeping the old-fashioned vibe intact.

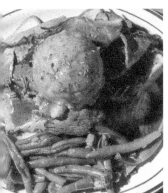

Left: Homecooked meals welcome diners to The Nashville House. *Center:* Enjoy outdoor dining on the patio. *Right:* The building that houses the restaurant was built in 1859.

Now the next generations—Andy's daughter, her husband, and their children—are keeping the traditions alive.

The rustic interior and great stone fireplaces create a warm ambiance that makes you long for days gone by. An outdoor patio space welcomes visitors to soak in the sunshine while they enjoy their hearty meal.

While there's a plethora of good down-home country-style Hoosier favorites on the menu, the most popular by far is the famous Nashville House Fried Chicken. It's a recipe that has been handed down for three generations. The crispy house-fried chicken is served with mashed potatoes and smothered in rich gravy made in-house and accompanied by a serving of fresh green beans.

Allow time to peruse the shelves in the general store, where you'll find homemade jams, local honey, baskets, walking sticks, and wooden toys. And of course, you'll need some foodie souvenirs, like homemade jams, local honey, and oven-fresh breads, pies, cookies, and other baked goods.

15 S Van Buren St., Nashville, 812-988-4554
nashvillehousebc.com

DUNES PAVILION

Dine steps from the sand overlooking
Lake Michigan

The building that houses the Dunes Pavilion Rooftop Restaurant and Grill is getting close to the century mark. But it's not just its age and architecture that make it so unique. It's also its location. Set in the Indiana Dunes State Park, it's surrounded by sand and water with stunning views. It's the only dining spot on the water for many, many miles and the only one in Indiana where you can sit and sip wine with that unique perspective of seeing the Chicago skyline in the distance and blue water as far as the eye can see.

The Indiana Dunes State Park opened in 1926, preserving the unique flora of the dunes for future generations as industry was filling in other parts of the Northwest Indiana shoreline. At least a quarter century earlier, talk of establishing the dunes as a national park was first considered, but it would be well over a century until that finally came to be.

When the state park was created, plans began for construction of a facility to serve visitors of the park and beach. In 1929, construction began at the cost of $100,000 on a two-story Indiana Dunes Pavilion to serve as a bathhouse and restaurant with a fine-dining room, restrooms, concessions and a rooftop observation deck. As we moved into the 21st century, the building had gradually deteriorated and was used only for a small concession stand, a lifeguard office, and storage. The Art Deco–

> You do pay an entrance fee to enter the park, even if you are there simply to dine. So, make the most of it with some swimming, bird-watching, or hiking. You can even opt to do overnight camping.

Left: The view from the Dunes Pavilion rooftop as the sun sets over Lake Michigan. *Center:* The historic beach house built in 1929 is where the Dunes Pavilion is now located. *Right:* The rooftop has beautiful views of the Indiana Dunes and Lake Michigan.

style building was crumbling and its future was uncertain considering the funds that would be needed to bring it back to its original condition.

A public-private partnership project is what it took in the end to make the restoration happen. In 2022, after years of renovation work, the Dunes Pavilion reopened as a restaurant, event venue, and rooftop lounge by Pavilion Partners.

Keeping with the original design, it was restored replicating original windows and other features. The structure is once again a shining gem of the Indiana Dunes where people gather and memories are made. Gallery walls on each floor cover the history of the Dunes. It is open seasonally with lighter fare that matches with a day on the beach in the hot sun. The Pavilion Cafe and a general store occupy the first floor with grab and go freshly made burgers, hotdogs, pizza, ice cream and more. The second floor is an event space holding up to 175. The rooftop is the jewel of the structure where you can sit for causal bites and cocktails, ordering through QR code and seating yourself. The taco concept gives vacation vibes with tacos as the main feature along with a Green Chili Burger, chips and dips and a fajita salad. There's no better place to say cheers than on the rooftop while the sun sets over Lake Michigan. It's something every Hoosier needs to experience at least once.

1600 N 25th St. E, Chesterton, 219-250-2568
dunespavilion.com

ZAHARAKOS ICE CREAM PARLOR AND MUSEUM

A museum and eatery all in one

The year was 1900. The second Olympic Games opened. The World Exhibition was taking place in Paris. The British Labour Party is officially established. Queen Victoria is in the 63rd year of her reign. The first Zeppelin airship flight takes place. And, in Columbus, Indiana, a little candy shop called Zaharakos opened.

Zaharakos has become one of the oldest ice cream parlors in the country, founded by Greek immigrant brothers James, Lewis, and Pete Zaharako. Originally a confectionery, the soda fountains were added after the brothers saw The Liquid Carbonic Company display at the 1904 St. Louis World's Fair. They purchased two Mexican onyx soda fountains and added them in 1905 and 1911. They also purchased a Tiffany-style lamp/carbonated water dispenser that was on display at the fair and placed it at the front of the bar. In 1908, a German-made Welte orchestrion mechanical pipe organ was ordered for $5,000. And in 1911, a 50-foot dark grained mahogany back bar with stained glass was added along with a 40-foot counter of Mexican onyx and Italian marble.

James's five sons worked in the shop in the 1930s and took it over in 1945. Some of them managed it for the next few decades before it went on to a third generation. Financial difficulties and declining health led to the closing of the shop in 2006. That's when Columbus businessman Tony Moravec decided to restore this historic gem. It now operates again as an ice cream parlor that also serves as a museum filled with old soda fountain equipment and music machines. It has the largest collection on public display of pre-1900 soda fountains. In

Left: Make sure to venture over to the museum side to view a second vintage bar and soda fountain equipment. *Center:* A classic banana split is a popular menu item. *Right:* The signature sandwich at Zaharakos is the GOM, made with their own classic beef and pork sloppy Joe recipe and grilled on soft Texas toast. Be sure to add American cheese.

restoring the site, Moravec purchased the contents of Jahns ice cream parlor in New York and expanded with vintage pieces. An orchestrion still operates when you insert a quarter.

When you order an ice cream treat, you are still getting premium ice cream that is made fresh on-site in one of their eight flavors. They also serve a brownie sundae, a banana split or their signature dessert, "The Big Z," which features five oversized scoops with three sauces, whipped cream and cherries.

Although ice cream is the focus, they also have a sizable lunch and dinner menu, and the item that you must try is their signature sandwich, the GOM. This sandwich has classic Zaharakos sloppy Joe made from beef and pork with a blend of spices on grilled soft, Texas toast with your choice of cheese (American is the usual addition). Pair it with a fountain soda made with syrup and carbonated water dispensed from the 1904 onyx soda fountain. You can select one of 13 syrups or combine flavors—including Coke, vanilla, cinnamon, cherry, root beer, red raspberry, and more. Taste it just the way they did in the early days.

329 Washington St., Columbus, 812-378-1900
zaharakos.com

A fun fact is that during World War II, Zaharkaros became self-service due to a shortage of staff.

RESTAURANTS A-Z

8Eleven Modern Bistro
201 S Grant St., Ste. 100
West Lafayette, IN 47906

950 Speakeasy Bistro
950 Washington St.
Lagro, IN 46941

**1875: The Steakhouse
at French Lick Resort**
8670 W SR-56
French Lick, IN 47432

Abbott's Candies
48 E Walnut St.
Hagerstown, IN 47346

Adams Street Chophouse
617 E Adams St.
Muncie, IN 47305

Albano's
119 S Calumet Rd.
Chesterton, IN 46304

Asparagus
7876 Broadway
Merrillville, IN 46410

Ballard's in the Atrium
8538 W Baden Ave.
West Baden Springs, IN 47469

Bao's Pastry
12 Jefferson St.
Valparaiso, IN 46383

Bluebeard
653 Virginia Ave.
Indianapolis, IN 46203

Blue Gate Restaurant
195 N Van Buren St.
Shipshewana, IN 46565

Blue Top Drive-In
8801 Indianapolis Blvd.
Highland, IN 46322

Cammack Station
9200 W Jackson St.
Muncie, IN 47304

Catello's Italian Art Cuisine
103 E State St.
Pendleton, IN 46064

Chicory Café
105 E Jefferson Blvd., Ste. 103
South Bend, IN 46601

Cindy's Diner
230 W Berry St.
Fort Wayne, IN 46802

Das Dutchman Essenhaus
240 US-20
Middlebury, IN 46540

Desserts by Juliette
401 S Main St.
Kouts, IN 46347

Destination 814
814 Detroit St.
LaGrange, IN 46761

Dunes Pavilion
1600 N 25th St. E
Chesterton, IN 46304

El Taco Real
935 Hoffman St.
Hammond, IN 46327

Farina's Supper Club
3311 Pottawattomie Trl.
Michigan City, IN 46360

Firehouse BBQ & Blues
400 N 8th St.
Richmond, IN 47374

**Fort Wayne's Famous
Coney Island Wiener Stand**
131 W Main St.
Fort Wayne, IN 46801

Goshen Brewing Co.
315 W Washington St.
Goshen, IN 46526

Henry's
536 W Main St.
Fort Wayne, IN 46802

Hostess House
723 W 4th St.
Marion, IN 46952

Iechyd Da Brewing Company
317 N Main St.
Elkhart, IN 46516

Iozzo's Garden of Italy
946 S Meridian St.
Indianapolis, IN 46225

Ivanhoe's
979 S Main St.
Upland, IN 46989

John's Famous Stew
1146 Kentucky Ave.
Indianapolis, IN 46221

Joseph Decuis
191 N Main St.
Roanoke, IN 46783

Junk Ditch Brewing Company
1825 W Main St.
Fort Wayne, IN 46808

Little Italy
1155 Joliet St.
Dyer, IN 46311

Long's Bakery
1453 N Tremont St.
Indianapolis, IN 46222

**Macri's Italian Bakery & Trattoria
and Carmela's at Macri's**
214 N Niles Ave.
South Bend, IN 46617

Mayberry Cafe
78 W Main St.
Danville, IN 46122

Merrillville Tea Room
7005 Madison St.
Merrillville, IN 46410

Miner-Dunn
8940 Indianapolis Blvd.
Highland, IN 46322

Mishkenut Mediterranean Cuisine
221 Ridge Rd.
Munster, IN 46321

Montego Bay Grille
322 Main St.
Hobart, IN 46342

Moser's Austrian Cafe
201–203 E Michigan St.
New Carlisle, IN 46552

Mrs. Wick's Pies
100 N Cherry St.
Winchester, IN 47394

Mug-n-Bun
5211 W 10th St.
Speedway, IN 46224

Nick's English Hut
423 E Kirkwood Ave.
Bloomington, IN 47408

Nick's Kitchen
506 N Jefferson St.
Huntington, IN 46750

Oasis Diner
405 W Main St.
Plainfield, IN 46168

Old Colonial Inn
216 N 3rd St.
Kentland, IN 47951

One Eyed Jack's
124 N Market St.
Winamac, IN 46996

Payne's Restaurant
4925 S Kay Bee Dr.
Gas City, IN 46933

Perillo's Pizzeria
5 S Broadway St.
North Salem, IN 46165

RH Indianapolis
4501 N Michigan Rd.
Indianapolis, IN 46228

Rock-Cola Cafe
5730 S Brooksville Rd.
Indianapolis, IN 46219

Root & Bone
4601 N College Ave
Indianapolis, IN 46205

Rusted Silo
411 N State St.
Lizton, IN 46149

Santa's Candy Castle
15499 N SR-245
Santa Claus, IN 47579

Schnitzelbank
393 3rd Ave.
Jasper, IN 47546

Shapiro's Delicatessen
808 S Meridian St.
Indianapolis, IN 46225

South Side Soda Shop
1122 S Main St.
Goshen, IN 46526

St. Elmo Steak House
127 S Illinois St.
Indianapolis, IN 46225

St. James Restaurant
204 E Albion St.
Avilla, IN 46710

Story Inn
6404 IN-135
Nashville, IN 47448

Teibel's Family Restaurant
1775 US-41
Schererville, IN 46375

**The Farmhouse Restaurant
at Fair Oaks Farms**
754 N 600 E
Fair Oaks, IN 47943

The Hulman
141 E Washington St.
Indianapolis, IN 46204

The Nashville House
15 S Van Buren St.
Nashville, IN 47448

The Overlook Restaurant
1153 W SR-62
Leavenworth, IN 47137

The Port Drive-In
419 N Calumet Rd.
Chesterton, IN 46304

The Prewitt
Restaurant and Lounge
121 W Main St., 1st fl.,
Plainfield, IN 46168

The Rathskeller
401 E Michigan St.
Indianapolis, IN 46204

The Super Burger
600 W Main St.
Paoli, IN 47454

The Taco Dive
1452 119th St.
Whiting, IN 46394

The Tin Plate Fine Food
and Spirits
2233 S J St.
Elwood, IN 46036

The Workingman's Friend
234 N Belmont Ave.
Indianapolis, IN 46222

Tippecanoe Place
620 W Washington St.
South Bend, IN 46601

Triple XXX Family Restaurant
2 N Salisbury St.
West Lafayette, IN 47906

Twenty
111 W Market St.
Wabash, IN 46992

Tyler's Tender
350 E US-30
Schererville, IN 46375

Union Hall Restaurant
at Journeyman Distillery's
American Factory
258 S Campbell St.
Valparaiso, IN 46385

Valpo Velvet
57 Monroe St.
Valparaiso, IN 46383

Vera Mae's Bistro
209 S Walnut St.
Muncie, IN 47305

Whistle Stop
Restaurant & Museum
10012 US-421
Monon, IN 47959

Zaharakos Ice Cream
Parlor and Museum
329 Washington St.
Columbus, IN 47201

APPENDIX

MICHIANA

INDIANAPOLIS METRO AREA